DO YOU KNOW YOUR RIGHTS?

Maurene J. Hinds

CENSORSHIP

PRIVACY

DUE PROCESS

ZERO TOLERANCE

CONSTITUTION

FREEDOM

Enslow Publishing
101 W. 23rd Street
Suite 240
New York, NY 10011
USA

enslow.com

GOT ISSUES?

Published in 2016 by Enslow Publishing, LLC
101 W. 23rd Street, Suite 240, New York, NY 10011

Library of Congress Cataloging-in-Publication Data

Hinds, Maurene J.
  Do you know your rights? / Maurene J. Hinds.
    pages cm. — (Got issues?)
  Audience: Grade 9 to 12.
  Includes bibliographical references and index.
  ISBN 978-0-7660-7193-3
  1. Parent and teenager—Juvenile literature. 2. Children's rights—Juvenile literature. 3. Teenagers—Legal status, laws, etc.—Juvenile literature. I. Title.
  HQ799.15.H56 2016
  305.235—dc23
                    2015028088

Printed in the United States of America

To Our Readers: We have done our best to make sure all website addresses in this book were active and appropriate when we went to press. However, the author and the publisher have no control over and assume no liability for the material available on those websites or on any websites they may link to. Any comments or suggestions can be sent by e-mail to customerservice@enslow.com.

Portions of this book originally appeared in the book *You Have the Right to Know Your Rights: What Teens Should Know.*

Disclaimer: For many of the images in this book, the people photographed are models. The depictions do not imply actual situations or events.

Contents

What Are Your Rights?

In September 2009, a student, "G.C.," was caught texting during school, a violation of the Kentucky school's policies on cell phone use. The teacher took his phone and gave it to the assistant principal, who then read through other text messages on the phone. The student had been involved in prior disciplinary issues, and the assistant principal claimed that she read through the other messages to ensure G.C. wasn't planning to hurt himself or someone else. The student was expelled.

G.C. and his parents sued the school and argued that the search was a violation of G.C.'s Fourth Amendment rights. The Fourth Amendment protects "The right of the people to be secure in their persons, houses, papers, and effects, against unreasonable searches and seizures, shall not be violated, and no Warrants shall issue, but upon probable cause, supported by Oath or affirmation, and or things to be seized."[1] In this case, the family argued that when the assistant principal read through other messages, it was an "unreasonable search and seizure" of G.C.'s private information, even though the event took place during school.

The case made it to the United States Court of Appeals, where it was determined that G.C.'s rights were, in fact, violated, both for the expulsion and the search of his phone. In the explanation of the case, the court stated, in part, that, ". . . using a cell phone on school grounds does not automatically trigger an essentially unlimited right enabling a school official to search any content stored on the phone that is not related either substantively or temporally to the infraction."[2] In other words, the school took the issue too far by searching personal information on the phone after confiscating it from the student.

This case helped pave the way for both students and schools regarding rights related to emerging technology. Schools have a responsibility to keep students safe while respecting the rights of minors.

Minors are people under the age of eighteen. In most states, eighteen is the age at which minors become adults with most legal rights. These include the right to vote and to serve in the armed forces. Other rights also become legal at this age, such as the right to enter into a contract.

Certain basic rights are sometimes called human rights. These have less to do with the law. These are what some people think are rights basic to all humanity. An example is the right to live in a dignified manner. For example, many people do not consider slavery to fit the definition of dignified. As a result, many people think slavery is a serious violation of human rights.

This resource discusses issues about both legal rights and human rights. It also covers a number of questions related to rights. Do minors have rights? Should they have rights? If so, which ones?

Who controls those rights? Is it lawful and ethical (good or right in conduct) to restrict rights of persons under eighteen?

Until fairly recently, children had few rights even in the United States. The law considered children property of their parents. This meant that parents could treat their children however they saw fit. This could include physical harm. Parents could hit their children or even sell them into slavery. Over time, however, parents and others began to see children as people. They saw that children had rights and were not property. Still, even today, many children around the world do not have the same rights as children in the United States.

Throughout history, issues of human rights have evolved. This can be seen in examples of uprisings against oppressors, revolutions, and wars. The United States' history grew out of the oppression the founders tried to escape. The Revolutionary War released the colonists from British rule. Later, the enslavement of African Americans became an issue of human rights and led to the Civil War. Over time, the Industrial Revolution gave rise to many changes in the way Americans did business. Dangerous work and long working hours led workers to revolt and demand changes. The world discovered Hitler's horrors during World War II. After this, human rights became even more of an issue around the world.

In 1948, the United Nations developed the Universal Declaration of Human Rights (UDHR). This document listed what the organization considered to be basic human rights. These included the right to life, security, freedom of expression, and education. The articles of the declaration are not law. They do serve as a guide for all nations on human rights issues. But not all nations agree that these are basic human rights. Even people in the United States do not all agree on what human rights are or should be. Those nations that agree with the declarations set forth by the United Nations pledge their support by first signing the articles. After signing, they ratify them, meaning those nations formally and legally agree to the articles.

It was not so long ago that children in the United States were subjected to inhumane labor conditions, such as working long hours in dim, airless factories.

Former First Lady Eleanor Roosevelt was a driving force in the creation of the Universal Declaration of Human Rights. Roosevelt worked for the rest of her life to ensure these rights would be acknowledged in the United States and around the world.

Some critics argue that the UDHR was developed from ideas out of Western culture. They argue that the articles do not consider Eastern countries' ideals. The articles are supposed to be universal. But many of the rights listed actually go against some people's views on government. Some Asian countries, for example, place a high emphasis on societal values rather than individual values. But some of the rights in the UDHR promote individual rights first. This is offensive to those who disagree. The United States has criticized China for its human rights violations. One famous example occurred in 1989 in Tiananmen Square, Beijing. A group of university students protested against the Communist government. They wanted democratic reform. After about a month and a half of protest, the Chinese government used the army to clear out the demonstrators. As the students left the square, violence erupted in the streets. The police killed many protesters. Some critics of the UDHR argue that many Western countries still have human rights violations of their own to correct. These critics would like to see a human rights agenda that is more universal.

John Shattuck, a former US assistant secretary of state, wrote an article called "Civil and Political Rights in the United States." In it, he writes, "Human rights have come to be recognized as the universal birthright of every man, woman, and child on this planet."[3] On November 20, 1989, the United Nations adopted the Convention on the Rights of the Child (CRC). This outlined specific rights for children around the world. The CRC defines children as anyone under the age of eighteen. The Convention lists fifty-four articles about children's rights and how to put the rights into action. The articles include discrimination issues and the right for children to speak out on their own behalf. It says children should be able to voice opinions about what is best for them. Two other optional rules added later deal with children in the armed forces and child pornography. The United States signed the convention, but the Senate did not vote to ratify the articles. Somalia is the only other UN country that has not ratified the CRC. There are a few reasons for this. One reason is that the United States has traditionally placed a high level of importance on the rights of parents to determine what is best for their children. The United States argues that a set of rules may interfere with a parent's right to make decisions.

Another reason the United States did not ratify the CRC is that the articles say the death penalty for anyone under eighteen years of age is a violation of human rights. Before 2005, some states allowed the execution of minors; other states did not. Then, in March 2005, the Supreme Court held in Roper v. Simmons that executing minors was unconstitutional. It is not yet known whether this change will affect the US position on the CRC.

Other reasons the United States refused to ratify the CRC include the convention's policies on economic, social, and cultural rights. The United States has long recognized political rights, such as free expression and the right to assemble, but it has been slower in recognizing issues such as the right to education, health care, and decent standards of living.[4] People in the United States continue to debate these issues. While there is no formal right to an education, for example, minors must attend school up to a particular age. This age varies by state, which leads to the final issue of why the United States has not ratified the CRC.

Each state is responsible for making its own laws, as long as those laws do not violate the Constitution. Because of this, many laws vary from state to state. If the government ratified the CRC, the states would have less power to determine their own laws. This goes against how the United States government is set up.

Why focus on children's rights? Many human rights groups treat children's rights as its own issue for one reason: to give children a voice. Some children are stuck in abusive situations, poverty, or are forced to work against their will. Someone needs to speak out for them because children cannot do it for themselves. Many violations of children's rights still occur around the world today. Some continue in the United States. The issue of children's rights is big and covers the globe. This book focuses on the rights of minors in the United

Children deserve to have a voice. Many who need help cannot speak for themselves. This is why the issue of children's rights is so important and widely debated. Do you know your rights?

States. Even here, the issues are many and cannot be covered in one book. This book is a sampling of some of the issues that children and adolescents in the United States face. It also discusses laws that have come from or changed children's rights issues and the current state of these issues.

Minors and the US Constitution

The Bill of Rights protects citizens' rights in the United States. These are the first ten amendments to the US Constitution. Additional amendments have been added over the years. Each state also has its own constitution, which must not be in violation of the US Constitution. Many cases involving constitutional rights result in litigation, or a lawsuit. The state and federal courts decide most cases. However, the only purpose of the United States Supreme Court is to deal with cases involving the Constitution. If a person is not happy with a decision of a state's highest court, he or she may ask the Supreme Court to hear the case. This can only be done if the issue is one that is directly related to the US Constitution. Some laws are different from state to state. These include laws that affect human rights issues. In these situations, the Supreme Court may refuse to hear the cases because they should be decided at the state level.

How does this process work? The Supreme Court reviews the lower court's decision. It then decides if it will hear arguments on the case. Nine justices sit on the Supreme Court. Each justice votes on the issue at hand. A majority vote will determine the case. If the justices do not all agree, each side will write a statement, or opinion, explaining their reasons. Often one justice will write this, speaking on behalf of the others on the same side. Sometimes more than one justice will write an opinion. This depends on his or her views on the subject. The Supreme Court does not act like other courts. There is no jury and no witnesses testify. Arguments for or against a person's innocence are not presented. Lawyers only argue whether or not a person's constitutional rights have been violated.

State courts have decided many cases involving children's rights. Sometimes these cases have prompted a change in state law. Other cases have made it all the way to the Supreme Court and brought about a change in the laws across the country.

The Right to Free Speech

In the United States, citizens have the right to express their views even if those views are seen by some as being incorrect or even offensive. Free speech is granted to all even if the viewpoints of some are considered by many to be wrong. However, even this freedom has some limits, and those limits may be further limited for teens, depending in part on where and when someone decides to exercise their rights.

Expressing oneself may mean many different things to different people, but regardless of the viewpoint, expression has its limits. This is true even in a country that protects freedom of speech and freedom of expression.

Can a person say whatever he or she wants? Yes and no. Saying certain things may result in a problem with the law. Using swear words in public may violate a local law on disturbing the peace. Threatening to kill the president, whether in speech or in writing, is a federal offense. Other threatening speech, however, is allowed. Physical harm against another person is illegal. But US citizens are able to say what some consider hate speech. Hate speech is when a person expresses hatred toward another group of people. Many regard hate speech as offensive, but it is still legal in many cases. People have the right to their opinions and to express those opinions. It does not matter how others may feel about those opinions. As long as the person does not act in a hateful way, which could be a crime, that person is allowed to express his or her views.

Some types of speech are intended to cause damage, however. Defamation of character is the legal term that describes when one person tells lies about another person that are meant to damage that person's reputation or otherwise cause harm. The defamed person has the right to sue the person who is saying the slanderous or false things.

Additionally, the First Amendment does not protect threatening speech. This is speech that contains threats against a person or a person's property. In these cases, lawyers try to show in court that most people would consider the speech a serious intent to do bodily harm or assault. Then, the person making the threats may be found guilty of breaking the law.

Expressing oneself through personal appearance also has some limits. How a person chooses to physically express him- or herself seems almost limitless. The law, however, does draw the line with some behaviors. These include showing parts of the body in public, such as women's breasts or either gender's genitals, and some sexual conduct.

Religious expression also has some limits. The founders of the United States wanted to make sure the government did not officially support any religion. As a result, US citizens enjoy the freedom to practice any form of religion. As with all rights, religious expression is okay so long as it does not violate another person's rights, well-being, or health. However, some religious practices are illegal. This includes intentional cruelty to other people or denying medical care to a person in need.

Teens have many of the same rights of expression that adults have. But these rights are limited at a public school.

Rights at School

Some people have argued that young people's rights should not remain outside the door when they attend school. However, public schools have the duty to ensure the safety and well-being of all students. As a result, some rights that are legal outside of school have some limits inside the classroom. This includes some rights of expression. Students have the right to express themselves in school as long as that expression does not harm another person. It also cannot interfere with the school's goal of education.

The classroom and extracurricular activities can provide a good way for students to discuss issues, express opinions, and develop a sense of identity and self. For example, in 1965, Mary Beth Tinker, thirteen, along with her brother, John, fifteen, and friend Christopher Eckhardt, sixteen, wore black armbands to protest the war in Vietnam. Their school, which had recently banned armbands, said they were a "disruptive influence" and could lead to a student protest. The school suspended all three students. Mary Beth and her family sued the school. They argued it was a violation of the students' First Amendment rights. The case, *Tinker v. Des Moines*, ended up in the Supreme Court. There, the justices agreed with the students in that the statements of protest were not disruptive and did not violate the rights of other students. The students had First Amendment rights to express their opinions. In the words of the Court:

> First Amendment rights, applied in light of the special characteristics of the school environment, are available to teachers and students. It can hardly be argued that either students or teachers shed their constitutional rights to freedom of speech or expression at the schoolhouse gate.[1]

However, there are some types of speech or expression that are not allowed in school that are legal outside of school. For example, schools do not put up with hate speech. The school has the power to limit it despite a person's constitutional right to free speech. The purpose of hate speech is to create emotions and strong reactions. Such speech in school would disturb the classroom setting and the goal of learning. Just as in the otuside world, schools do not allow students to tell lies intended to harm the reputations of other students. This is true for both verbal and written remarks.

Should students have the right to wear whatever they want on school property even if it is considered offensive by the school administration?

What Are the Current Laws?

Public schools have the power to decide what is okay and what is not regarding students' appearance. Private schools have even more control in this and other areas. Schools may ban anything they think will get in the way of the goal of learning. Various court cases on this topic have ended up with different rulings. In 1966, the case that set the tone for hairstyles in public school took place in Dallas, Texas. Phil Ferrell, Paul Jarvis, and Steve Webb were members of a rock band. They decided that growing their hair long would help to promote the band. The principal of their school, however, disagreed with this idea. He told the students they could not attend their senior year of school unless they cut their hair. The state court agreed with the principal. It ruled that the school, not the students, had the authority to make the rules. If the school can show that a form of expression is getting in the way of other students' ability to learn, then the school may curb that behavior. This can include such things as wearing gang-related colors or clothing, religious symbols, or T-shirts with advertising or other messages. Schools may also limit extreme makeup or hairstyles. Some schools decide to use school uniforms to help avoid problems with clothing. If everyone is wearing the same thing, students will not be distracted by messages on T-shirts or worrying about not having the "right" clothes.

Issues concerning students and dress or personal expression continue to make the news as schools try to determine what is acceptable within the school setting and what is not. In March 2014, a student at Grand Island High School was suspended for wearing a National Rifle Association T-shirt.[2] In the spring of 2015, several stories made the news of students who were disciplined because of prom dresses that were deemed too revealing.

A school may also not show special treatment for one particular religion over another. This is why prayer in schools has gotten so much attention. Schools may allow a moment of silence. This does not lend itself to one particular religion over another. But reading a prayer out loud in class or over the loudspeaker is not allowed. This

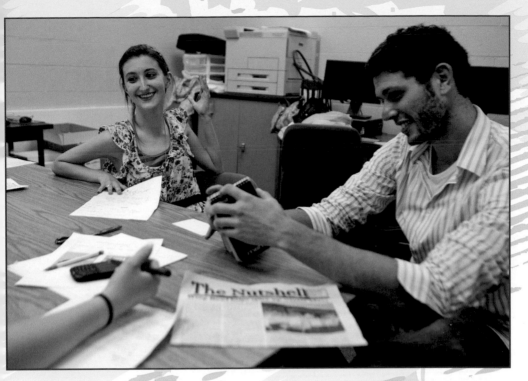

Should a school administration have the right to control the editorial content that goes into a student-run school newspaper? The Supreme Court has ruled that it should.

would be showing support of certain religious beliefs. Schools do not allow prayers at graduation ceremonies for the same reasons. Students have the right to attend school and school functions without being exposed to religious beliefs or statements.

In a 1988 case, *Hazelwood School District v. Kuhlmeier*, the Supreme Court ruled that a school could control the content in school newspapers. This is because school newspapers are not a forum for public expression. This particular case dealt with stories in which students expressed personal opinions about a family divorce, teen pregnancy, sexual activity, and birth control. Some of the quotes used names of the persons interviewed. While other quotes did not, students would have been able to guess the person quoted. The principal removed two pages from the paper. He decided that if the paper went to print with the content he removed, it would be a violation of the right to privacy of both students and their parents. The Supreme Court agreed.[3] Students may not say or write whatever they wish in school. While school papers may be an excellent source to express opinions and debate issues, some topics may be off-limits. Schools have the power to prohibit material considered improper. This power may not be in violation of students' rights.

Free Speech in Schools

Has anyone opposed these laws? Most of the challenges to the law or school policies are the result of specific incidents. They are not the result of groups trying to change the laws in general. Most of these cases involve a person arguing a violation of his or her constitutional rights. Despite general laws, specific cases may or may not be a violation of a student's constitutional rights.

Should there be laws that forbid hate speech? Some argue yes, some argue no. Speech shown in court to be a real threat of physical harm may result in criminal charges. But under the First Amendment, people of the United States have the freedom to express their opinions. Some reasons for arguing against hate speech laws are that hate speech is too unclear and difficult to define. What one person considers hate speech may not be to another person or group. Another risk of having hate speech laws is that they may work against the minorities or victims at whom hate speech is often directed. These groups need the freedom to respond to hate directed at them. They need the freedom to make their voices heard and bring attention to the hate problems in the first place. Laws or restrictions against hate speech could actually have the opposite effect, opponents say.

Naturally, hate speech offends many people. Some worry that such speech will lead to actions against the targets of such speech. Hate speech gives rise to many emotions. These emotions can lead to heated arguments, physical harm, and riots. Hate speech carries a high level of emotion. It also serves to threaten the targets or bring an audience to action. Because of this, schools may limit such freedom of expression.

In 1962, the Supreme Court heard a case on prayer in the school system, *Engel v. Vitale*. The New York State Board of Regents had approved a prayer that students recited daily in New York schools, "Almighty God, we acknowledge our dependence upon Thee, and we beg Thy blessing upon us, our parents, our teachers and our Country."[4] The Regents claimed that the prayer was not associated with any particular religion. Some parents in one school district decided that the prayer was unconstitutional and violated the rights of students. New York state courts first heard the case. It decided that the school system operated within its legal limits. The Supreme Court disagreed and used the Establishment Clause as part of its argument.

The Establishment Clause is one of two clauses under the First Amendment that deal with the issue of religion and government. The amendment prohibits the government from declaring or funding any particular religion. This had happened in other countries.[5] For example, England had a long history of conflict between Protestants and Catholics. For a long time, whichever religion the ruling king or queen supported became the national religion. In its decision on Engel v. Vitale, the Supreme Court wrote:

> The constitutional prohibition against laws respecting an establishment of religion must at least mean that in this country it is no part of the business of government to compose official prayers for any group of the American people to recite as a part of a religious program carried on by government.[6]

The decision was controversial then, and it continues to be so today.

Both those who support prayer in public schools and those who oppose it use the First Amendment for their argument. Those who support school prayer argue that the amendment does not allow the government to prohibit religious expression. The amendment states, in reference to religious expression, ". . . or prohibiting the free exercise thereof." Those who argue against school prayer say that the government cannot encourage one religion over another. Because prayer is often associated with a particular religion and because public schools are government-supported institutions, they say prayer should not be allowed.

In 1992, the Supreme Court decided in *Lee v. Weisman* that school prayers were not proper at a junior high graduation ceremony. In this case, the school had a policy that allowed for a prayer at graduation. The rules stated that the prayer needed to be nondenominational. Deborah Weisman, who graduated in 1989, did not feel that students should be forced to listen to a prayer at a school function. She and her family sued the school. The case eventually ended up in the Supreme Court. Deborah and her family won the case. The Justices ruled:

> A government may not coerce anyone to support or participate in religion or its exercise, or otherwise act in a way which "establishes a [state] religion or religious faith, or tends to do so." [7]

The Court also said:

> That the directions may have been given in a good-faith attempt to make the prayers acceptable to most persons does not resolve the dilemma caused by the school's involvement, since the government may not establish an official or civic religion as a means of avoiding the establishment of a religion with more specific creeds. [8]

The school prayer issue has come up again and again since these decisions. The debates continue. However, these rulings, at least for now, have set the standard for prayer in school.

The debate over whether prayer should be allowed in public schools rages on. Some people believe it is not appropriate, and others believe students should have the right to pray in school if they wish.

Does this mean that no religious activities can occur on the school grounds? No. Many schools have clubs or groups that are based on students' religious beliefs. The difference is that involvement in these groups is by choice. No students are required to attend. The school's primary responsibility is to provide educational opportunities for all students. This includes keeping order in the classroom and among the student population in general. This does not mean that hot topics cannot or will not be discussed in the classroom. Schools are a great place to discuss all sides of an issue. But the school does have the right to place limits on its students.

Social Media and School

What students do on their own time is their own business, right? Not necessarily. With social media being a big part of many students' lives, the lines between what happens in school and what happens outside of school have blurred. Posts made by students outside of school and cyberbullying are examples of concerns that have caused schools to create policies related to social media. Because of the severity of some issues, many state laws have also been put in place to help protect students and their rights.

Students have been suspended and even expelled for posts they have made on Facebook, Twitter, and other social media sites. Freedom of expression is a right; however, that expression can cross a line, which can lead to more serious consequences. Posts that contain illegal information, are meant to cause harm (bullying), are threatening, that speak poorly of others (defamation), or anything that is against a school's policies can get students into trouble—not only in school, but also with the law. These types of posts may be violations of free speech.

In 2011, a student in Minnesota was expelled for a year after he posted a list on Facebook. He titled the post "Hit List" and included the names of thirty school staff, students, and graduates. The list caused concern even though no other specific threats were included in the post, aside from the title. However, the student's parents were notified, as were the local police.[9] In early 2015, a Tennessee teen was suspended for more than a year—past her expected graduation date—as a result of a Twitter conversation. In the posts, no specific person was named, but the school determined the messages were threatening, including, "I would kill her." She was not charged by police, but the school's zero tolerance policy and suspension prevented her from enrolling in a different public school.[10]

Another student's senior year was disrupted by a two-word Twitter post in which he responded to a question about whether or not he had made out with a teacher. The student said that his sarcastic response, "Actually, yeah," was not meant to be taken seriously. However, he was ultimately suspended for several days for threatening and intimidating a teacher, despite apologizing. The student was never charged with a crime, although he and his parents did sue the school district and the district police. He transferred to a different school and noted that the incident ruined his senior year. [11]

Aside from potential legal and school troubles, posts can be problematic for minors in other ways, also. Posts, photos, and other information that may put a person in a negative light can cause problems later on. Information that is put on the web essentially stays on the web forever. Even if someone deletes a photo or post, there is no guarantee that someone else did not copy the post or photo or share it with others. People have had trouble finding jobs because of online posts—even years later. Information sent by text or email can be shared by the receiver with anyone at any time without the sender's knowledge. ProtectMyRep.org is a project by ThreeSixty, a youth journalism program at the University of St. Thomas in St. Paul, Minnesota, that aims to help young people use social media responsibly and in ways that will help avoid future problems.

One potential problem is information being shared by others. Anyone can take a photo or video and post it online. If the photo or video shows someone doing something embarrassing or even illegal, problems can result. While everyone makes mistakes, trying to avoid situations that can be potentially embarrassing may help avoid future problems. Minors need to be careful about what they post. By not posting embarrassing, harassing, and otherwise controversial information, minors help protect themselves.

The digital age has created a unique set of issues when it comes to free speech, personal rights, and the right to privacy. Some feel that school policies and laws have gone too far in limiting free speech. Others see some of the tragic consequences of cyberbullying and feel that not enough has been done. Finding the right balance is an ongoing issue.

Cyberbullying and the Law

As the earlier example shows, a two-word Twitter post, meant in jest, has the potential to land a teen in trouble. Many experts agreed that the student's suspension for that post was extreme. But what happens when social media posts are not meant to be taken lightly, and are instead intended to cause harm? Cyberbullying has become such a problem that most states have laws in place to help protect victims of online bullying.

Stopbullying.gov defines cyberbullying as "bullying that takes place using electronic technology. Electronic technology includes devices and equipment such as cell phones, computers, and tablets as well as communication tools including social media sites, text messages, chat, and websites."[12] Cyberbullying can include "mean text messages or emails, rumors sent by email or posted on social networking sites, and embarrassing pictures, videos, websites, or fake profiles."[13]

One reason cyberbullying is particularly problematic is because it can happen at any time. The Internet does not turn off, and bullies have access to their targets outside of school and other in-person locations. As a result, a person can be a victim in his or her own home or any other location that is supposed to be a safe place. The effects of cyberbullying (and other types of bullying) can be severe, including physical symptoms, a lack of sleep, changes in habits, a lost interest in attending events, lower grades, feeling helpless, lowered self-esteem, and self-destructive behaviors including running away, self-harm, and even suicide. [14]

Because cyberbullying is an increasing problem with several stories making the news with tragic outcomes, both schools and the legal system have gotten involved. Many schools have policies related to the use of social media sites and technology both inside and outside of school. The majority of states have some type of law or policy in place related to bullying. StopBullying.gov provides a map of the US showing which states have laws or policies in place. The map can be viewed at www.stopbullying.gov/laws/index.html.

Anyone who is a target of bullying, cyber or otherwise, has the right to feel safe. Steps that targets of cyberbullies can take include blocking the offender, saving and printing the offending messages or photos to use as evidence, talking with a trusted friend or adult, and if the bullying includes threats or other harmful messages, reporting the information to school officials and law enforcement.

When Rights Are Violated

Unfortunately, there is no one way to handle a case about freedom of expression. Each situation is different. The laws vary from state to state. For many teenagers, these events are likely to occur within the school setting, but this is not always the case. Other issues to think about are where and how suspected violations occur. For example, can a teen be banned from shopping in a grocery store with Hispanic owners if the teen made racist remarks while in the store? In this case, yes, because the store is a privately owned business. But what if the teen makes similar remarks in a public library? This may depend on the situation. If the remarks are disruptive to other patrons, the librarians may ask the teen to leave. The patron could face suspension from using the public resource for a set amount of time. What if the conversation takes place privately and a Hispanic librarian overhears the conversation and is offended? Can the library throw out the teen? Probably not because the conversation only took place between the two people involved.

Events such as these may be treated differently than those that occur at school. If necessary, students may report an incident to the police. Often, though, people who feel their rights were violated will start by talking to a lawyer. The lawyer will then advise those involved on what actions to take. Lawyers may file a lawsuit on the person's behalf against the other party. Cases are often settled out of court through a shared agreement. Other times, however, cases go to court. These may end up in the Supreme Court.

In school, most issues will be reported to school officials or the school board. Many issues can be solved without having to pursue the matter further. Sometimes this does not work. It may be necessary to seek legal help and possibly take the case to court. Students have as much right as anyone else to guarantee the protection of their rights in or out of school. Students who stood up to the rules and asked for change have caused courts to support some of the rights of students. These cases brought public attention to the rights of children and teens. Not everyone agrees with the results, but it is the basis of constitutional protection that everyone has the opportunity to fight for his or her rights, regardless of age.

Rights at Work

Many teens look forward to the opportunity to apply for and work a part-time job. The rewards can be many, including extra income, a sense of self-reliance and responsibility, gaining experience, learning new skills, meeting new people, and building a list of references. Both adults and minors have rights in the workplace. However, minors are more restricted in some areas than adults, including when they can begin working, how many hours they are allowed to work each week, and the types of jobs they can perform.

Until recently, children and teens had no rights in the workforce. During the Industrial Revolution, children often worked twelve- to fifteen-hour days six days a week. The law did not require breaks, and many children worked all day without rest or with only a few short breaks. Business owners would punish workers they thought were not working hard enough. These punishments could include physical force or a cut in pay. Children spent hours bent over machines in textile factories. Unsafe working conditions were common. Children worked with dangerous machinery on a regular basis. People of all ages were seriously hurt and even died while on the job.

In the United States and several European countries, however, conditions began to change in the nineteenth century. Laws now protect minors from abuses in the workplace. In many parts of the world, conditions are changing, as well. Child labor issues are a major concern among human rights groups. Despite progress, child labor is still a major concern in some parts of the world.

Other laws affect all workers, not just children and teens. It is important to have an understanding of these laws before entering the workforce.

Workplace Rights

Even before hiring someone, employers may not ask some questions either on applications or in an interview. Questions about a person's race or religion are not legal in most cases. Questions about age can also be illegal. An employer may ask if the job seeker is legally old enough to work, but employers cannot ask for a date of birth or why a person is seeking work at this age. Employers may not ask about relationship status. An employer may not ask if the applicant is seeing anyone nor if the person is married. Employers may ask a person about prior felony convictions. But employers may not ask about a person's history of arrest or if he or she has been in trouble with the law. Many older teens may seek delivery jobs. In this case, an employer may ask if the person has a valid driver's license. An employer may also ask if an applicant is a member of any clubs or organizations that may be relevant to the job. They may not ask an applicant to list all clubs or organizations of which he or she is a member.[1]

It is also smart to read the application carefully, especially the fine print. Applicants may be giving up some rights when signing

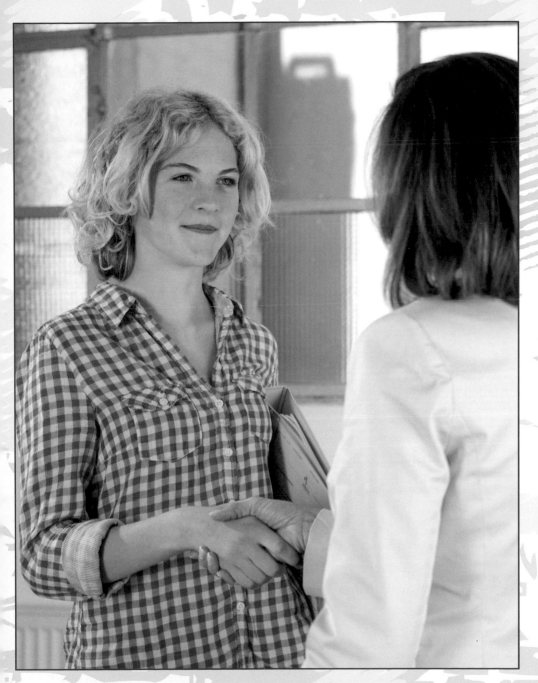

No matter where you work or what kind of job you have, you have rights in the workplace. In fact, you have certain rights even before you are hired by an employer.

the application. It is important to understand the agreement. Most importantly, an applicant must never exaggerate his or her history or lie on an application. These actions can lead to immediate firing. This is true even if the employer does not discover the lie until after the person has worked for a long time in the position.

An employer has to fulfill certain legal duties for all employees, not just minors. These vary somewhat from state to state, but there are some similarities across the country. For example, employers must provide a safe place to work. Some jobs are hazardous. Employers must provide safety and health training and provide information on any chemicals that are used. Employers must follow the rules of OSHA. This stands for the Occupational Safety and Health Administration. OSHA is a government agency that regulates workplace safety. Many workplaces must also provide workers' compensation insurance. This insurance covers injuries or illnesses that occur if a person is sick or injured on the job. Most jobs must also pay the minimum wage. This may not be the case with jobs such as waiting tables. Tips from customers provide a large part of the income from restaurant work.

Laws, Limits, and Labor

Certain age limits determine what type of work a minor may do. Age may also determine how many hours a minor may work each week. The 1938 Fair Labor Standards Act covered some areas of child labor. Those under eighteen years of age cannot work in some dangerous jobs. These include logging, mining, and work with dynamite or dangerous chemicals. However, the allowable age for working in some other jobs is lowered. These include delivering newspapers, babysitting, or working in the family business.

While each state determines its own labor laws, there are guidelines from the federal government. Students may not work during school hours. In general, students may not work more than forty hours per week during the summer or eighteen hours per week during the school year. They cannot work more than three hours

Student-age workers enjoy particular rights. Employers may not ask them to work during school hours, and they may not require them to work more than a certain number of hours per week.

per day. Students may work between 7 a.m. and 7 p.m. during the school year. Minors may not work graveyard, or overnight, shifts. Each state has its own rules about how late teenagers can work during the summer. Usually it is no later than 9 p.m. Many minors work later than this, especially in restaurants and cashier positions. Some states also place limits on age for door-to-door sales. Some have rules about minors working in the entertainment business, for instance as actors or models.

Teens also have duties in the workplace. All employees need to understand the job and what employers expect of them. Employees must follow safety and workplace rules. Just as teens do not want their rights violated at work, it is also important that a teen not violate the rights of other employees. Harassment in any form is against the law. Employers may fire employees for drinking or using drugs. Respecting other employees and their rights will help support a positive, safe working environment for everyone involved.

Teens may find some employment laws unfair. The laws are in place to protect minors from unsafe and abusive work environments. It was not long ago when children worked long days with little or no break. In poor families, students dropped out of school so they could work. In other parts of the world, children still work long hours with little pay and in unsafe environments.

Some people believe that not allowing minors to work puts unnecessary financial stress on some families. Around the world, many families could not survive if the children did not work. But

If you suspect that your employer is creating an unsafe working environment for you, look up your state's labor laws online. You can consult with a represpresentative from OSHA, as well.

children who work full time are not able to go to school. This means they will have little chance of getting better paying work later on in life. It is a tough cycle. Labor laws involving children in the United States began in the nineteenth century to help prevent this. In most states, children are required to attend school up to at least eighth grade. This helps ensure that most children receive a basic level of education. The limits on hours worked during the school year are in place to support education. They help make sure that minors are able to continue their education and work at the same time.

Teens who have dropped out of school are an exception to some labor laws. They may work full time. They also have the benefits that come with working full time. However, wages for a person who has not finished high school are much lower than those who at least have a high school diploma. Unemployment rates are also much higher for those who have dropped out of high school. A 2014 report shows that the unemployment rate for high school dropouts is just more than 30 percent while the rate for those who have completed high school is just more than 20 percent.[2] While dropping out of school to work may seem like a good idea, in the long run it can cause more problems than it has benefits.

When Rights Are Violated

Workplace abuses take many forms. Each situation needs to be reviewed on its own. Most workplaces have complaint procedures in place for employees to use if there is a problem. Some employers have better complaint policies than others. These procedures should be included in the employee handbook, if available. Sometimes workplaces are small and informal with no official complaint policy. How to deal with an issue depends on the work environment. Ideally, the first place an employee will turn to report or discuss a problem is his or her supervisor.

Anyone who suspects that an employer is not following the law has the right to report that employer to the proper authorities. Report workplace safety issues to OSHA or to the state's workers' insurance plan. Employers are required to post information on state insurance coverage and agency contact information. Do an online search. Use workers' compensation and the state name for information on each state's workers' compensation plan. An employee may feel that the work environment is unsafe and causes immediate danger. He or she has the right to refuse to work until the employer corrects the problem. On average, about seventy teens die from work-related injuries each year.[3] Many more are injured every year.

Agriculture and working alone with cash are the two most dangerous jobs for teens.[4] Teens working agricultural jobs have died or been seriously hurt from the tools used. Sadly, teens have also died working alone late at night in jobs that require working with cash. These types of jobs include restaurant and cashier positions. Employees also have the right to join or organize a union, though not all employers support unions. In addition, no one needs to put up with sexual or other harassment on the job.[5] Harassment is when one person troubles or annoys another over and over or makes constant attacks. Sexual harassment occurs when these activities include comments about sexual activity, obscene remarks, or inappropriate touching.

If a supervisor is harassing an employee, the employee will need to take other steps in reporting it. Sometimes there is only one boss. In this case, an employee may need to report a complaint to someone outside of the business. Problems can be discussed with an attorney. Other organizations to contact include the local job service, which is a state-run agency that assists people in finding jobs and explaining local labor laws, or the Better Business Bureau. Public reference librarians can also help find a proper agency. There are a number of organizations to contact about workplace issues. Employees can report health and safety issues to OSHA and the state's workers' compensation offices.

Purchasing Power

Teens generally gain more freedoms as they grow older, and one of those freedoms is access to their own money and making purchasing decisions. As a whole, teens are a source of billions of dollars, as this group has access to money but few bills to pay. Advertising and sales companies are aware of this and specifically target this age group, or demographic, often before minors reach the teen years. If a company can hook a young buyer, it may be able to turn that buyer into a lifelong customer.

Advertising seeks to influence certain groups of people. Look at the difference between ads run during Saturday morning cartoons and those shown during prime time in the evening. Ads run during the middle of the day target stay-at-home moms. Ads run during programs for teens also attempt to attract and hook the audience.

Advertisers also target young buyers in not-so-obvious ways. Product placement is a common method. It puts products in

Advertisers know exactly how to target teens by creating a desire to have the latest and coolest clothes and gadgets. Regardless of your age, it is important to know your rights as a consumer.

television shows, movies, or video games in such a way that it seems to be a part of the setting but, in fact, is a method of advertising. Teens may be aware of product placement, particularly when it is seen all over a video game. Even with this awareness, however, some teens fall victim to the advertising anyway. About a skateboarding game, one teen said, "You see a board in the game that you like and you want the equipment . . ."[1]

What about product placement in schools? Some large companies, such as those that make soft drinks, will help support school programs. They give schools money in return for the school putting vending machines on the premises. Other companies are not quite as subtle. Some school educational tools use or show a product name or picture as part of the learning material itself. Why would a school choose to use such educational material? Companies provide the material for free or at a low cost. Many schools' budgets are tight. All consumers, not just teens, need to be aware of the methods used by advertisers.

When teens do decide to shop, they may face problems that most adults would not face. For example, retail employees or security officers may be more likely to keep an eye on a teen shopper than they would an adult shopper. While teens spend a lot in retail, business owners often see them as problem shoppers. The Mall of America, for example, put a policy in place in 1996, which has since been revised, that required adult supervision of teen shoppers. This meant shoppers sixteen years of age or younger must be accompanied by an adult age twenty-one or older after 4 p.m. on Fridays and Saturdays until closing time.[2] The policy was initially put in place because the mall had become a hang out. The mall security workers said the groups of teens were causing problems. The mall also developed a youth advisory council. This council worked with the mall staff to help figure out solutions for the kids that hung out at the mall. The council broke up in 2000, but it helped bring a voice to teen shoppers.[3]

Young Consumers' Rights

Minors do not have some consumer rights. This includes the right to enter into certain types of contracts. However, everyone has the right to not be conned by companies. Some sellers use unethical or illegal means of getting someone to purchase a product or service. Those who use illegal methods sometimes do not even have a product or service to offer. How can teens protect themselves against such practices? By knowing their rights, being aware, and using a healthy amount of skepticism when it comes to advertised promises that seem too good to be true.

As consumers, teens have the right to protect themselves against scams. To avoid scams, there are some things that teens need to be aware of. One is modeling scams. Ads may promise huge salaries and no upfront costs. But the contract given to the potential model asks him or her to pay hundreds of dollars for photos. The agency claims they will use the photos to promote the model. Legitimate modeling agencies, however, usually collect fees by taking a percentage of the fees paid to the model. Payment is made only after the agency has found work for the model. Many agents work this way. A valid modeling agency may ask for the model to pay for printing costs for a picture in the agency's book. The costs for this type of promotional material are small and only cover the model's part of the printing cost. Potential models also need to be wary of agencies that claim to represent all types of people. These agencies lead some people to believe that they may have a career in modeling when this is, in fact, unrealistic. Valid modeling agencies do not work with all types of people. Scam artists do, and they charge all types of people, as well. Fake scholarships are another area students may fall prey to. Most legitimate scholarship programs do not require an application fee. Most also have strict guidelines. Those that do require a fee and have loose procedures and requirements may be scams. It is also wise to avoid paying for scholarship-searching services. They are unreliable. If a scholarship program looks doubtful, a high school guidance counselor can help figure out if it is legitimate. So also can the financial aid office of the college or university.

Health scams are another area teens should be aware of. The culture in the United States (and elsewhere) is obsessed with being thin and muscular. Numerous diet programs, pills, powders, drinks, and exercise programs promise fast results from using their products. Often these products are highly priced. They also often require that the user continue taking the product for a long time. This ensures long-term sales. Some diet or exercise programs require that participants sign up for a long period of time. They also add on hidden costs after the fact. This can include paying for food, supplements, or equipment. Many clubs and services have the clients sign contracts that lock the person into the agreement for a long time. This could be years. The bottom line is that even safe, legal pills cannot make people thin. Almost all of the advertising for these products include fine print. The fine print says diet and exercise are an essential part of any weight loss program. It is not possible to spot reduce, or lose weight or fat from one specific area of the body, through exercise. If a promise or claim seems too good to be true, it probably is.

When Problems Arise

The law does require certain things of both buyers and sellers. Consumers need to report problems within a realistic amount of time. They also need to keep accurate records to prove how much, when, and how they paid for something (cash, check, or credit card). If copies of contracts and selling agreements list rules that the seller agrees to, the consumer should keep all that information on file.

What products do teens have the right to buy? Under pressure from the public and possible legislative action, the entertainment industry has voluntarily used rating systems for such items as video games, CDs, and movies. Various states have passed laws about selling certain products to minors. Movies are rated G for general audiences; PG, meaning parental guidance is suggested; PG-13, meaning some material may not be suitable for persons under the age of thirteen; R for restricted, meaning that anyone under age seventeen must be accompanied by a parent or adult guardian; and NC-17, meaning no one under seventeen is allowed. Other types of entertainment use different rating systems. The Entertainment Software Rating Board (ESRB) rating systems are the most common for video games. These rating categories include Early Childhood, Kids to Adults, Teens, Mature, and Adult Only. The Recording Industry Association of America (RIAA) developed a parental advisory label for music. Television uses a set of guidelines ranging

Even though you are afforded certain rights, be a smart consumer. Read the fine print, use your critical thinking skills, and keep detailed records. Remember, if it sounds too good to be true, it probably is.

from Y, which is suitable for all children, to MA, which is for mature audiences only.

The nation continues to introduce legislation about how companies market products to minors. Laws also affect how businesses display products and the outcomes of selling unsuitable material to minors.

How are labels viewed? Minors and parents will probably continue to disagree about certain labels. Parents and the entertainment industry will probably continue to disagree on some labels, as well. But a recent study showed that parents and the industry are coming together in some areas. Parents wanted rating labels. The media voluntarily used ratings—although it was under threat of possible legislative action. The study states, "When an entertainment industry rates a product as inappropriate for children, parent raters agree that it is inappropriate for children."[4] In other words, the entertainment industry and parents agree on what is, or is not, appropriate for minors. The study also explained the need for both parents and the entertainment industry to take responsibility for exposure to minors. The study, "A Validity Test of Movie, Television, and Video-Game Ratings," recommended that a universal rating system be developed. This would eliminate different rating systems for different forms of entertainment.[5]

What about shady companies and scams? Rules exist for them, too. Sweepstakes, for example, must follow certain rules to remain legal. They must provide the entrant a business name and contact information. They must also list the estimated odds of winning, the dollar amount or retail value of a prize, and payment schedules. It is illegal for sweepstakes to announce that a person has won when he or she has not. Nor can they imitate government seals or require a purchase to win. Be careful of high shipping costs on free items. These should sound a warning bell for the consumer.

Movies, television shows, and music now come with ratings that caution parents about content that may not be suitable for teens and children. But do minors have the right to decide for themselves?

Speaking Out

Some consumer laws that deal with minors are being challenged by groups that support youth rights. These include the American Civil Liberties Union (ACLU), kidSPEAK!, and the Youth Free Expression Network. These groups work not only to change the labeling laws as they relate to music, movies, and games, but to also have most age-related laws done away with. These people believe consumer rights should extend to all people regardless of age. They feel that young people can and should make their own decisions on how they spend their money. Some groups want to see all information and entertainment that is available for adults made available for minors, as well. Groups such as these also push for a lower voting age, no drinking age, and so on.

On the other hand, many people support the labeling of music and games, as well as the limitations on adult material, such as pornography. They argue that they are protecting young people. Some people argue that violent games promote violent behavior. They point to such cases as the Columbine High School incident. The boys involved in the school shooting were also fans of violent games. People who support music labeling believe that sexually explicit lyrics and those promoting violence are not suitable for minors.

Critics of labels argue that minors should be able to choose what they watch and listen to just as adults do. How do the artists feel about labels? According to the Teen Consumer Scrapbook, some artists say they appreciate the labels. The labels help families and also help prevent censorship of the artist's work.[6] Do the labels work? A 2004 report by the Federal Trade Commission (FTC) stated that most industries were obeying the labeling guidelines. However, the report also said the music, movie, and video game industries were still advertising the mature-rated products in ways that reached a younger audience, such as ads in magazines and TV shows that kids are exposed to.[7] The FTC's concern is that the industry is specifically targeting children despite labeling on those products saying they are for older consumers only. The industries may be complying with the voluntary guidelines, but a more important issue is whether or not minors are still able to purchase the products. The report states, "despite the existence of restrictive policies among some retailers, the Commission continues to find that teens can purchase rated or labeled entertainment products at a significant number of stores and theaters."[8]

Taking Action

Sometimes a product is defective or a customer needs to return an item. Most retailers want to keep customers happy. They will work with those who have complaints or wish to exchange or return merchandise. As long as the customer's complaints are reasonable, many businesses will exchange defective products or issue a refund. Some will take back merchandise with no questions asked. Some businesses sell services rather than products. Many of these will work to correct the problem rather than risk an unhappy client. Upset clients tell their friends about the poor service.

Unfortunately, not all businesses are so easy to work with. How does one go about complaining? Teen Consumer Scrapbook is an online site for teens created by teens. It shares knowledge on commercialism and provides tips for teens when it comes to dealing with difficult businesses. Some of their suggestions include:

- Complain as soon as possible, and be clear with the facts of the issue. When writing, calling, or complaining in person, it is important to have all the information on hand to answer questions and present a case. Information that may be required are the date of purchase, amount of purchase, a receipt of purchase, serial and model numbers, warranty information, and other related information.
- If the first attempt is unsuccessful, try using a different approach. If the first complaint was through a phone call, for

example, complaining in person or by a letter may have better results. It can also help to ask to speak with a supervisor.

- Ask for a specific remedy and time frame, and use a firm voice and words.
- Follow up after the complaint. If no action is taken to resolve the problem, further action may be needed.[9]

If the complaint is with a large company or is the result of a suspected scam, it may be necessary to start at a higher level. The Better Business Bureau and the Federal Trade Commission are two agencies that deal with consumer issues. They also provide a wealth of information for consumers on their websites. Suspected scams and other consumer complaints can also be reported to the state auditor's office.

Health and Well-Being

One's health is obviously a personal issue, as are decisions related to one's health. These decisions relate to physical, emotional, and mental well-being. Teens face additional stress from changing bodies, emotional ups and downs, and concerns about their future. These issues can be a lot to deal with; when additional challenges are added, some teens may find themselves feeling overwhelmed and unsure.

As with adults, teens have a right to the pursuit of happiness, which includes physical and mental well-being. This also means teens have rights when their safety and overall health is at risk.

Parents and guardians have a responsibility to take care of their children's health needs and provide the healthiest environment possible. Unfortunately, this is not always easy due to the high costs of health care and insurance, as well as food and shelter. Sometimes a parent's failure to provide health care and a healthy environment for their children crosses the legal line. This can even result in parents losing their rights to have their children live with them.

Two areas that can result in adults losing their parental rights are abuse and neglect. Abuse can be emotional or physical. It is difficult to prove emotional abuse to the point where a parent would lose rights. Physical abuse, as it relates to parent and child, occurs when the parent physically harms the child. This can include hitting or shoving. Sexual abuse occurs when an adult engages in sexual behavior with a minor. Neglect occurs when parents or caregivers do not meet the needs of their children. This is usually intentional. In some cases, a parent's mental illness will cause them to neglect a child. Either abuse or neglect can result in the loss of parental rights. Parents are required to meet their children's physical needs. They must also provide health care as needed. But can a teen seek health care without a parent's consent? Sometimes.

Typically, many doctors and health care providers will not treat a minor without the consent of a parent or guardian. However, most states allow teens to seek medical care for certain issues. These include drug and sexual health issues, outpatient mental health, pregnancy care, and in some cases, abortion. These are serious issues that require immediate assistance. As a result, most doctors do not deny care on the basis of parental consent.

If a teen's health is in immediate danger, doctors will give care without consent. An example of this is a serious accident where the patient could die or suffer serious injury if immediate medical care is not given. In other less obvious cases, a doctor can still provide care without a parent's consent. If a teen has a drug problem and seeks treatment, his or her parents do not need to be informed. A teen can also seek information on reproductive health and sexually transmitted diseases (STDs). But the lines become blurry when teens seek treatment for STDs, pregnancy, and abortions. The laws differ from state to state on whether parents should be notified or required to provide consent.

Health Care Choices

Teens have the right to seek health care and get accurate answers to their questions. Medical care is not limited because of a person's race, religion, age, or gender. Seeking medical help without a parent may seem a little frightening. Even if a parent is not present, the teen, as the patient, deserves treatment with dignity and respect. If this does not happen, the teen may need to find another health professional or organization. The patient also has the right to ask to see his or her records and have any confusing information explained.

Many aspects of health care can be overwhelming. Patients are required to fill out forms—often more than one. Many procedures and conditions have long confusing names. Teens have a right to know what they are signing. They also have the right to understand what all procedures and tests are and their purpose. If a health care worker is not explaining things well, it is okay to ask to have the information repeated in common language. Often medical language does not make much sense. Health care workers need to explain medical terms in understandable words. This happens to both teen and adult patients. Once the patient fully understands the information, he or she has the right to refuse any medical procedures. Following tests or procedures, the patient has the right to know the results. While seeking medical treatment can at times feel intimidating, it is important to speak out and ask questions.[1]

Legal Issues

If a teen's health is in serious danger, he or she may seek medical treatment without parental consent. Special options are available for those seeking treatment for alcohol or drug dependency. Options are also available for those seeking treatment from abuse. Teens needing help for sexually transmitted diseases may seek medical care without the consent of a parent.

States have differing laws on when parents need to be informed or provide consent on health care issues. Minors may buy over-the-counter contraceptives just like any other consumer. In some

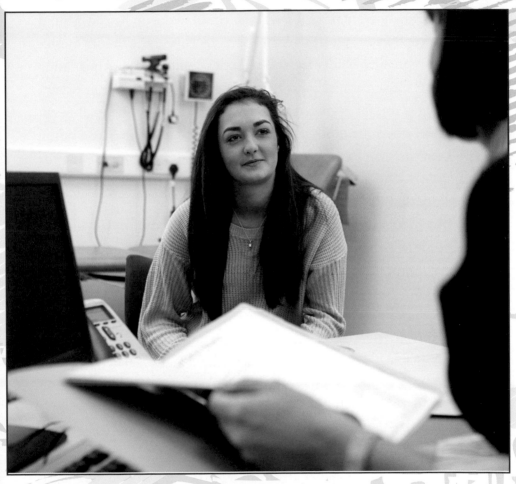

While minors generally need a parent's consent to be treated by a health practicioner, they do have the right to seek care for certain medical issues.

states, minors may also be able to obtain prescription birth control methods without a parent's knowledge.

Girls who are seeking an abortion have special rights. *Roe v. Wade*, a 1973 landmark Supreme Court case, ruled about a woman's right to an abortion. It said a woman could make up her own mind about whether or not to seek an abortion during the first trimester of her pregnancy. Under the ruling, states could pass laws regulating abortion during the second trimester. States could also pass laws protecting the fetus during the third trimester and only allow an abortion when the mother's health or life was in danger. The ruling was controversial and remains so today. Naturally, arguments for or against abortion for minors have continued, much the same as arguments about abortion in general.

What are the laws? Some states allow a minor to seek an abortion without informing her parents and without obtaining their consent. Others require that parents must be notified but do not require consent. Still others require consent. Obviously, this by its very nature requires notification. Arguments for each option are varied. Some people fear that if a teen must notify her parents— or parent; some states require only one parent be notified—or get consent then she will seek other unsafe methods for aborting the fetus. People who support notification and consent feel that a pregnant teen is unable to make the decision on her own. They believe parental involvement is in her best interest.

The Alan Guttmacher Institute reports regularly on state laws about minors and STDs, pregnancy, and abortion. According to the institute:

- 32 states require some parental involvement in a minor's decision to have an abortion.
- 18 states require parental consent; 2 require both parents to consent.

- 14 states require parental notification; 2 require that both parents be notified.
- All of the 32 states that require parental involvement except Utah have an alternative process for minors seeking an abortion.
- 31 states include a judicial bypass procedure, which allows a minor to obtain approval from a court.
- 6 states also permit a minor to obtain an abortion if a grandparent or other adult relative is involved in the decision.
- Most states that require parental involvement make exceptions under certain circumstances.
- 27 states permit a minor to obtain an abortion in a medical emergency.
- 12 states permit a minor to obtain an abortion in cases of abuse, assault, incest, or neglect.[2]

Minors may seek treatment for drug and alcohol use. When seeking treatment, the minor's records are kept confidential. This means that a parent cannot see the minor's records unless the minor gives written consent. The laws generally provide confidentiality. This is so those with drug or alcohol problems will not be scared off from seeking treatment. However, a doctor can share a minor's records with parents under certain circumstances. For instance, parents can be notified if a minor's condition poses a threat to his or her life, or that of someone else, and if the doctor believes informing the parents will reduce the threat. Finally, notification may be necessary if the minor is unable to make a good decision based on extreme youth or other mental or physical conditions.[3]

Minors may also seek mental health care without parental consent. There are two types of mental health care. One is inpatient care, where a hospital or care center admits the patient. The other is outpatient care, where the patient receives treatment by visiting caregivers, such as regular visits to the doctor. In most cases, minors can get this type of treatment without parental notification or consent. The age at which a minor can obtain mental health care treatment without parental involvement varies from state to state.

Health Laws

The laws about emergency situations, drug- and sex-related issues, and mental health issues exist because the states realize that these situations require immediate help. While some people do not like the laws, they are in place to protect young people. A minor's health is more important than the parents' wishes in some cases. Along with these laws is the need for confidentiality of medical records. The laws recognize that adolescents, particularly older teens, are at a point in their lives when they are making more and more decisions for themselves. Having the right to control some issues of personal health is important to this process. The laws also recognize that teens may need someone to talk to. This person must be someone that they can trust and whom they know will keep the conversations confidential. If a parent is not able to perform this role or if a teen does not trust a parent, a health care provider may be able to give the information and support that a teen needs.

Abortion, in particular, is an issue that evokes many emotions. People feel strongly about the issue. Some feel so strongly, in fact, that they have died for their beliefs. People who reject abortion under any situation reject it for teens, as well. Some groups will continue to push for laws outlawing abortion. These groups do not support abortion regardless of the age of the mother.

Other people who are usually opposed to abortion may not be opposed, or may be undecided, when it comes to teens. Some people may be uncomfortable with abortion generally but will support it if the mother's health is in danger. Some people may also support it in cases in which the mother is still in school, is unmarried, or is unable to care for a baby—all of which are more likely among teenagers than among older women.

There are also supporters of abortion who will continue to fight for keeping the practice legal. Many supporters worry about the effects of illegal abortions. They feel that women, especially young girls, will find other means of getting an abortion. These other methods are dangerous. Debates on the topic will continue. The age of the mother will also continue to be a factor in the discussions.

Seeking Medical Care

A teen in need of medical care may need it quickly. How does one go about finding such care?

Each state has its own laws about health care and teens. A good place to start asking questions is a family doctor. If a doctor is not available, your local Health and Human Services department

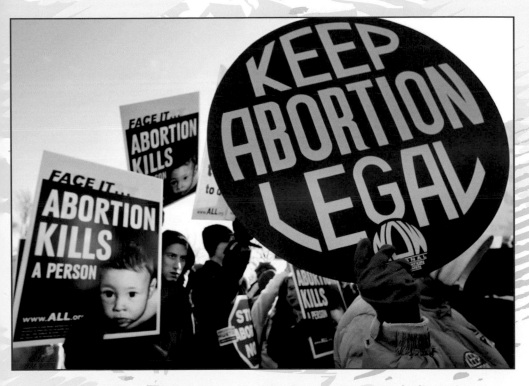

Abortion is a polarizing issue. Whether or not you believe in a woman's right to obtain an abortion, it is important to understand that the practice is legal in the United States.

can provide information. Do an Internet search for the contact information. Many communities have public health clinics that can help a teen find proper information. An emergency clinic may also have information. School counselors can provide local resources, as can reference librarians. If there is a local college or university, the on-campus clinic may also be able to provide information and services for attending students. Many college students are still minors. Many colleges have programs and information to help young people in need.

The Internet is another good resource for finding agencies. Search for general terms, such as alcohol counseling, to find treatment agencies and counselors who focus on family or child issues. A phone call can lead to much-needed information. Help is out there, and it can be found.

Drug Testing and Searches

Because drug use has become more of a problem in schools in recent decades, school administrators have searched for tools and methods to keep drugs out of schools. These include education programs and policies, as well as other more controversial approaches. Random drug testing has been used by some schools, but these tests are only used for students in extracurricular activities. Random unannounced searches are also used in some schools, where students' lockers, bags, and other personal items are searched. Proponents of these types of searches argue that they help keep drugs out of school. Opponents argue that these searches are ineffective and violations of students' rights, particularly when it comes to the Fourth Amendment.

In the workforce, drug testing is often required for jobs that are potentially dangerous. Examples are logging or those in which an employee is responsible for the lives or well-being of others, such as a commercial airline pilot. Some other jobs that involve a high level of responsibility or deal with confidential information may also require drug testing.

Schools face different situations. Should drug testing be limited to students who participate in athletics? Student athletes are much more likely to be injured if they are using illegal drugs. But is it fair to single out those students rather than testing the entire student body? In one well-known case that took place in Vernonia, Oregon, the school had a mandatory drug testing policy for student athletes. Jimmy Acton and his parents refused to sign the release allowing for the test. Jimmy argued that there was no reason to suspect he may be using drugs. Therefore, he did not think he should be tested. The school did not allow him to participate in the sports program.

Jimmy and his parents took the case to court. His case eventually ended up in the Supreme Court. Jimmy argued that he had protection under the Fourth Amendment. This amendment protects against unreasonable search and seizure. Jimmy argued that the policy invaded his privacy rights. The school district argued that drug use was prevalent in the school. They believed that the drug testing rules were legal and would help keep the student population under better control. Ultimately, the Supreme Court upheld the school policy. It said student athletes had fewer expectations of privacy. They change clothes and shower in the locker room, for example. The Court held that, because of the way the school gave the test, the collection of the urine sample was a limited invasion of privacy. Lowering drug use by athletes was more important than the athletes' individual privacy rights.

The Court's ruling was decided in a six-to-three vote. Justice Antonin Scalia wrote the Court's opinion, joined by Chief Justice William Rehnquist and Justices Anthony Kennedy, Clarence Thomas, Ruth Bader Ginsburg, and Stephen Breyer. The Court considered many factors in the case. It found that random drug testing of student athletes was not a violation of privacy. The justices said that participation in athletics was voluntary. The school was concerned about a drug problem among students. They said the testing was a reasonable search. The justices also said that students were required to submit to vaccinations. Athletes also had to submit to physicals before taking part in the athletic program. Students were also regularly subjected to other personal tests, such as those for hearing and scoliosis, a condition of the spine. The justices said "students within the school environment have a lesser expectation of privacy than members of the population generally."[1] The justices also discussed the negative effects of drugs. They said that random testing was for the overall good of the student population.

The dissenting justices included Sandra Day O'Connor, John Paul Stevens, and David Souter. They said that if the goal of the program was to keep the general student body under more control, the limited testing of just the athletes did not make sense. They argued that testing suspected drug users makes more sense. It is more in line with the law than random testing of all students, including those who have shown no signs of drug use. In other words, they argued that random testing of the entire student body—or even random testing among a specific group, such as athletes—includes students who have not given the authorities any reason to suspect drug use. This practice is a violation of those students' rights.

The dissenting justices said that random testing violates the rights of many more students than only testing those suspected of the offense. The justices said that in all other areas of the law, people do not undergo searches unless there is a suspected reason. They referred to situations outside of school. They argued that this should be the case in schools, as well. (Please note this case occurred before September 11, 2001; searches of the public have increased since those terrorist attacks.) This would also reduce the number of students exposed to privacy violations. The justices believed that a random or mandatory policy of testing the entire student body was not necessary. In fact, they felt that mandatory testing of all students would be a violation of their rights. Drug testing should be limited to only those suspected of use. The results should be limited to only those persons who needed to know, according to the dissenting opinion.

The dissenting justices said that drug testing was different from other procedures required by the school district, such as vaccinations. The justices said that the purpose of vaccinations is not to find something that may lay blame on the student. A student who receives a vaccination will not feel as if he or she is suspected of wrongdoing. However, that is the only response a student can have when asked to submit to a drug test, the dissenting judges argued.

The Fourth Amendment and School

Arguments about the constitutionality of drug testing often mention the Fourth Amendment to the US Constitution. This amendment protects a person against unreasonable search and seizure. However, some personal constitutional rights are waived in the school setting for the greater good of the entire student body. It is under this principle that many courts, including the Supreme Court, have upheld many drug testing cases in schools.

Does a student have the right to refuse a drug test? In the case of student athletes, one may refuse to take the test. This may result in not being able to participate in the sport. Because school athletics are not required, the drug testing rule does not interfere with the student's education.

If a drug test is performed, students have the right to be given the test in a respectful manner. A school official will supervise the test following certain guidelines. In the Vernonia school case, the person supervising the test needed to stand away from the urinal for boys. For girls, the person waited outside the stall. The sample was tested for temperature to make sure it was fresh. Only one person supervised the test, and the student's privacy was protected as best as possible. These were the standards already used in Vernonia, which the Supreme Court supported.

The courts also said that once test results are returned, the student has the right to know the results. Due to possible errors,

Whether or not your school or employer can insist that you undergo a random drug test depends on your state's laws and the circumstances. Knowing your rights can help protect you if you ever are faced with this situation.

students must be allowed to take a second test if the first one is positive for drug use. If the second test comes back negative, then the case is dropped with no further action taken against the student. If the student is suspended from school following a positive test, the school needs to inform the student of the reasons for suspension. Students also have the right to know that their sample will only be used to test for drugs that are specified before the test. The sample cannot be tested for medical conditions or pregnancy, for example. In 1975, the case of *Goss v. Lopez* determined that before a student is suspended, he or she must be made aware of the reasons for the suspension and given notice. Due process refers to the fairness in which laws are carried out. The Fourteenth Amendment to the Constitution protects due process. This amendment defines citizenship and guarantees equal protection under the law for all citizens.

Is It Legal?

So far, random drug testing for athletes, as well as students involved in other optional activities, has been upheld in courts because those activities are voluntary. In 2002, the Supreme Court gave schools more authority to randomly test for drugs among students who are involved in competitive or optional activities.[2] Later, in early 2004, President Bush announced plans to increase funding by $25 million for schools to use for random drug testing.

Random drug testing of all students and mandatory drug testing of all students or students involved in specific activities are not yet legal. Some believe that the United States is headed in that direction. In early 2004, a well-publicized raid on a school brought national attention. The raid took place at Stratford High School in Goose Creek, South Carolina. Its purpose was to find drugs. Police with guns and dogs entered the school. They searched students' persons, property, and lockers. While the incident did not directly involve drug testing, it drew national attention as the war on drugs continued. The American Civil Liberties Union filed a suit against the school on behalf of twenty families. They felt this was a gross invasion of privacy. No warrants were issued or warnings given to the students. It was deemed unreasonable by the parents—and no drugs were found.

Can schools search a student's person or possessions without a good cause? In 1985, the Supreme Court ruled on a case involving a fourteen-year-old girl. The assistant principal caught her and a friend smoking cigarettes in the school bathroom. Terry (known by her initials, T.L.O., in court documents) denied that she had been smoking. The assistant principal asked to see her purse. While looking through the purse, he saw some rolling papers, which he knew were used for marijuana. Upon a further search of the purse, the assistant principal found marijuana. He also found an index card that listed people who owed Terry money.

The principal called Terry's mother and the police. At the police station, Terry admitted to selling marijuana at school. She was then charged. In response, Terry argued that the search of her purse violated her Fourth Amendment rights against unreasonable search and seizure. A juvenile court heard the case. It upheld the assistant principal's actions. Terry then appealed her case through the court system. The Supreme Court eventually heard the case. The Supreme Court said the assistant principal had reason to suspect that Terry was violating school rules. She had been caught smoking, therefore the search for cigarettes in her purse was not unconstitutional. The rolling papers led to a reasonable suspicion that there might be drugs, as well. As a result of this case, school officials can search a students' person and property if they have a reasonable suspicion that a student is breaking or plans to break school rules. The decision must be based on a number of factors, including the student's age, history of behavior, and school records.

One and Done

Cases such as Terry's and more disturbing situations, such as school shootings, have led schools to become more cautious about what students bring into schools. This has led to zero tolerance policies. With these policies, schools do not allow any violations of the rules, no matter how innocent. The idea is to create an atmosphere where the school will not tolerate violations of the rules. This is to enforce safety and to ensure equal treatment among students in the process. Zero tolerance rules address all kinds of issues facing children in school. This includes weapons, sexual harassment, and drugs, both legal and illegal.

Another criticism of zero tolerance is the method in which the policies are enforced. Due process refers to basic rights, including substantive and procedural. Substantive rights are those that allow the individual the power to possess or to do certain things, despite the government's desire otherwise. These are rights such as freedom of speech and religion. Procedural rights are special rights that say how the government can lawfully take away a person's freedom, property, or life. Due process rights carry over to the school setting, as well. Many cases involving zero tolerance have to do with due process. In the T.L.O. case, for example, Terry argued that the assistant principal violated her constitutional rights when he searched her purse. She argued the search violated her due process rights—even though all the courts disagreed with her.

Zero tolerance policies grew out of a need to provide safe school environments. As long as schools continue to look for ways to reach this end, controversy over the methods will continue.

Too Far?

How far should school policies go? Many believe that plans for schoolwide drug testing go too far. Some people argue that many policies, particularly those of zero tolerance, cross the line and violate rights. Students have been suspended or expelled from school for using legal medications. These include over-the-counter medications, such as Tylenol, as well as prescription medications, such as asthma inhalers. States have been working on bills to allow children to carry their asthma medications in school. As noted on

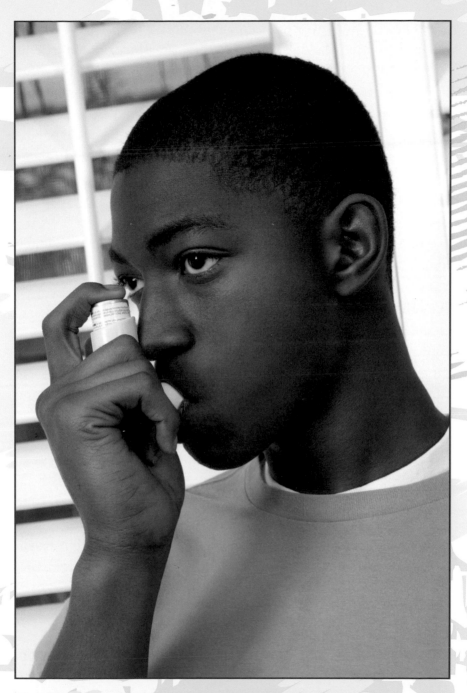

Many people believe that school antidrug policies have gone too far. If a student is denied much-needed legal medication, have his or her rights been violated? The answer may not be as simple as you think.

FindLaw, ". . . students who need medications administered to them during the school day already have legal possession (or their parents do) of any controlled substances. The school's role is therefore limited to ensuring safe custody, storage, and administering of the medication, once a valid authorization is received from parents/physician."[3] Schools set their own policies on how they will handle student medications and aim for a policy that will allow students who need access to medications to have it while also keeping the rest of the student population safe, particularly with prescription drugs.

Most people do not question the drug problem in the United States. Nor do they question that youth are at a risk for drug abuse. What is questioned is how the country is going about dealing with the drug problem and what schools are doing about it. It is difficult to determine exactly which policies go too far and violate students' rights to privacy and rights against unreasonable search and seizure. Does drug testing work and address the real problem? Some people believe that drug testing does not address the real issue. Good education about the harmful effects of drugs would do more good than random drug testing, they say. They argue that finding drugs in a urine test after the fact is not as useful as preventing drug use in the first place.

Not everyone views zero tolerance and strict drug testing policies as a violation of freedom. Drug abuse is common, and it causes many problems not only within the school setting but also in one's personal life. For the good of society, some people argue that drug testing is one way to help keep drugs out of schools.

But should a person's right to privacy and rights against unreasonable search and seizure be ignored because he or she is a middle or high school student? Supporters of student rights argue that these policies go too far. They argue that there are better ways to deal with drug problems. They recommend better education about drugs and their use rather than simply telling kids to "just say no" or using scare tactics. Just as with sex education, they argue, when teens know the specific facts, they are better able to make informed, reasonable, and educated choices.

Up for Debate

The courts have allowed schools more freedom when it comes to testing for drugs. But it is still up to the community and school to determine if there is a need for such testing. Whether or not a student's rights have been violated depends on each situation. Many issues are at stake. These include why the testing is done, how the testing is done, and what is done with the results. If taking a complaint about illegal drug testing to school officials or the school board is not effective or satisfactory, seeking outside legal help may be necessary.

Unlimited Data

Thanks to smart phones and similar gadgets, people of all ages now have access to unlimited types of information in the palms of their hands. While this availability of information can be useful, it has some downsides, as well. People are connected now more than ever. Any topic can be Googled, often with millions of results. The Internet can be a helpful tool. However, it also means that less helpful information, including information that parents and guardians may not want minors exposed to, may end up in the hands of children and teens. While some information may be viewed as inappropriate for minors, some of it is illegal for anyone to access.

Do teens have the right to access any information they are looking for? With the widespread availability of the Internet, all kinds of information is available. Anyone can put a website on the Internet. They can post information, regardless of qualifications or knowledge of a subject. Some of it is accurate. Some of it is not.

Should teens be prevented from viewing certain websites? What about posts and other content on social media sites?

Gathering, transferring, and sharing information can be a touchy subject. This is particularly true when it comes to the Internet. Some people want to require that certain websites be made illegal for minors to access. Some sites, such as pornography sites, are already illegal for minors. Websites containing information on how to build a bomb or that show graphic violence may fall into this category. Some sites already require that those who enter the site be eighteen years of age. But many sites do not require users to verify age. Therefore, some people want public institutions, such as libraries, to block certain websites that may be offensive to children or teens.

The American Library Association (ALA) has historically protected the rights of individuals to access information confidentially. This applies to both minors and adults. The association advocates the accessibility of information for everyone and maintaining the privacy of those who use libraries. Public libraries do not give out an adult patron's checkout history, for example. They will only do this if required to by law, such as when issued a court subpoena for certain records. If anyone, including government personnel, is allowed to review a patron's history, for example, it could have serious results. Libraries have different policies on allowing parents to access their children's checkout history. Some allow it up to a certain age. Some do not allow it at all. What if an abused child was looking into resources that could help him or her escape the situation? If the abuse came from a parent and the parent was allowed access to the child's records, it could have serious consequences for the child. Some states are looking into legislation that would make it legal for parents to access their children's records.

The ALA feels that what a person reads is his or her own business. According to the American Library Association, "Intellectual freedom is the right of every individual to both seek and receive information from all points of view without restriction. It provides for free access to all expressions of ideas through which any and all sides of a question, cause or movement may be explored."[1]

Because of this belief, many libraries do not use Internet filters on their computers. Filters may prevent patrons from accessing certain types of content, such as pornography, but the filters may block inoffensive or informational sites, as well. Filters work by looking for certain words. Someone seeking information on breast cancer, for example, could be denied access because of the word "breast." Some libraries use blocking software only on computers located in children's sections. Others do not use blocking software at all. However, it is illegal for a patron to expose a minor to sexually explicit material. If a person is caught doing so, he or she can face criminal charges.

With the rapid growth of the Internet and methods to access it over the past two decades, legislators introduced numerous acts with the purpose of protecting minors from unsuitable content. The Communications Decency Act (CDA) was introduced in 1996 and struck down by the Supreme Court in 1997 as a violation of the First Amendment. The CDA attempted to ban obscene or indecent information on the Internet. In *Reno v. ACLU*, the Supreme Court found that free-speech principles applied to the Internet. The Child Online Protection Act (COPA) was passed in 1998. Its purpose is to prohibit businesses from distributing harmful material, such as pornography, to minors. The Children's Online Privacy Protection Act (COPPA) went into action in 1998. It prohibits commercial websites from obtaining personal information from children under thirteen years of age. The Children's Internet Protection Act (CIPA) "requires libraries and schools to install filters on their Internet computers to retain federal funding and discounts for computers and computer access."[2] This legislation went into effect in 2000 and was updated in 2011. The Act links government funding to Internet safety policies. Essentially, libraries that are subject to CIPA's regulations need to have policies in place that provide safety

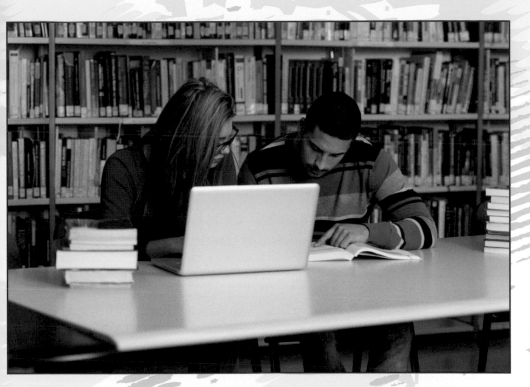

When using public libraries, you have the right to privacy regarding the content you access. However, libraries have the right to block pornography and other offensive websites from their computers.

tools regarding inappropriate material online, email, chat rooms, hacking, the disclosure of personal information, and methods to restrict minors to harmful materials.[3] While it is not required, some libraries feel they have no choice but to follow the rules to get the funding they need.

The ALA has continued to make changes based on the changing roles of libraries in the digital age. The organization continues to advocate intellectual freedom and maintains that parents have the primary responsibility to determine what their children can or should be exposed to, stating, "If parents want to keep certain ideas or forms of expression away from their children, they must assume the responsibility for shielding those children. Governmental institutions cannot be expected to usurp or interfere with parental obligations and responsibilities when it comes to deciding what a child may read or view."[4]

Privacy Rights

The Constitution does not specifically list the right to privacy. It is implied in the Fourth Amendment and, more recently, the Ninth.

While the right to privacy is not specifically mentioned in the Ninth Amendment, the courts have argued that this right is implied. The Ninth Amendment was created as a broad amendment to cover "rights of the people," and the right to privacy falls under this category. The Supreme Court rarely mentioned the Ninth Amendment until the 1960s, when it was used in a case in 1965 involving privacy for married couples (*Griswold v. Connecticut*). Since that time, the Ninth Amendment has been used in other cases about the right to privacy, as well.[5]

The Supreme Court has repeatedly made decisions that protect the privacy of individuals. But has it gone too far? Some people worry that the Court relies too much on the Ninth Amendment. They worry this allows the Court to invent rights and that it is gaining a power it was never meant to have. Traditionally, up until the mid-1960s, the courts used the Ninth Amendment only in conjunction with other amendments. This is because the wording of the Ninth is so vague. However, just because some issues have been argued and won using the Ninth Amendment does not mean that everyone agrees on the rights it implies.

Intellectual freedom issues fall under the First Amendment. Minors, like adults, have First Amendment rights. This includes the right to obtain information. Where and how information is obtained may vary from state to state and school to school. Minors have the right to look for information on a wide range of topics. Some people do not believe that minors should have access to all types of information even if it is legal for them to do so. This includes

The US Supreme Court was established by the US Constitution to be the highest court. Some believe it goes too far in its reach and has too much power.

information on sex, reproduction, and birth control. Censorship means keeping specific information from a person or group of people. Throughout history, information has been censored by many different people and institutions. Governments have censored information, as have other organizations and groups. Parents may censor information from their children, such as information on birth control. Our laws say they have the right to do so until the child reaches the legal age of eighteen. Parents may also require that their children be excused from reading certain material or learning lessons in school that they find offensive. This includes sex education classes and books that have been banned by some groups.

As far as book and Internet censorship are concerned, school libraries are more likely to limit information than a public library. Schools may limit information that does not support the goal of education. This broad definition can lead to censorship of material considered inappropriate, as opposed to simply educationally unsuitable. Schools may restrict some information if it is seen as vulgar. Who decides what is educationally unsuitable or vulgar? That is up to school officials. Outside opinions from the community or parents may also influence a school's decisions.

In 1982, in the case of Island Trees v. Pico, the Island Trees Union Free School District Board of Education acted to have some books banned from the school library. They considered the books to be "anti-American, anti-Christian, anti-Semitic, and just plain filthy."[6] Parents from the community disagreed with the decision, and the case eventually made it to the Supreme Court. The Supreme Court argued that "the Board could not restrict the availability of books in its libraries simply because its members disagreed with their idea content."[7] The Court found that the board's actions were in violation of students' First Amendment rights.

Some groups will continue to push to have books banned. A recent example of popular books that have faced criticism is the

Hunger Games trilogy because of the violence, language, and other content that some find unsuitable for young adults.

Access to Information

Laws about access to information and a person's records vary from state to state. When needed, the Supreme Court has weighed in on a few issues.

Minors' rights to receive information have been limited in two ways. The Supreme Court has given public schools the right to decide whether to keep certain information in the school or school library. The school can decide if the information is educationally unsuitable or pervasively vulgar. These are, of course, broad terms and are open to debate as to what they actually mean. The purpose of these terms is to leave the issue of information access up to school officials. This is to prevent one person's opinion, such as a teacher's, from unfairly affecting the decision.

On the other hand, this ruling gave schools a significant amount of control over the students' access to ideas and information. Public libraries are not under the same restrictions as school libraries. Most public libraries aim to stock the shelves and provide patrons with information that is geared toward the library's patronage. This can vary from library to library. Sometimes a public library chooses not to have particular information. This is often not out of a desire to keep information from the public, or censorship, but is more likely to be a result of funds and space available for material.

Whether or not there seems to be a community demand for such information also affects the decision. The Supreme Court has restricted information to minors that individual states may determine is obscene for minors but not for adults. This includes stores selling obscene material to minors. It also includes any other way in which minors may obtain obscene material outside the home. Many states have adopted harmful-to-minors statutes that dictate the laws on information access. It may be fairly easy for a school not to purchase obscene books or magazines.

Much of the controversy surrounding obscene material is the result of Internet access. The Internet can be a great learning tool, but it includes material that is not suitable for minors. Many people support the idea of censorship in the form of filtering programs on computers. They believe that it is a necessary safety measure to protect minors. Some useful information may be blocked. The overall usefulness of the filters is worth the loss of some information, they say. They believe that filters do more good than harm. Others argue that the filters block too much information—even for minors. They say it takes the idea of protection too far. Some words commonly blocked by filters include those that may help minors find important health information. This could include sexual health information or information on controversial topics, such as homosexuality. Some teens may be in desperate need of help and have no other source of accurate information. Filters may prevent them from finding it.

Staying Safe Online

The Children's Online Privacy Protection Act (COPPA) was created to protect minors on the Internet. The rule "imposes certain requirements on operators of websites or online services directed to children under 13 years of age, and on operators of other websites or online services that have actual knowledge that they are collecting personal information online from a child under 13 years of age."[8] The rule is designed to help protect minors from being taken advantage of or exposed to material that is not age-appropriate or is illegal. It also helps protect owners of legitimate websites by ensuring they remain within the law.

The law requires that websites cannot obtain personal information from a minor under the age of thirteen without parental consent. Parents also have the right to review any information provided and to remove that information if they choose. Schools are allowed to determine which websites are appropriate for class use, and many schools choose to provide students and parents with related policies about Internet use. Other schools require that students and parents sign forms agreeing to the policies to help ensure that students use the Internet and technology responsibly while they are in school, as well as when using these tools for school.

Minors also have the right to be safe from online predators to the extent that this is possible. Any pornographic information that involves a minor is illegal, and young people have the right to protect themselves. Online predators intentionally seek out minors. They will often pretend to be younger and may create fake online profiles. While victims of an online predator cannot be blamed, all users of the Internet can take steps to protect themselves.

The US Federal Bureau of Investigation (FBI) provides recommendations for parents about online safety. They suggest that parents tell children and teens:

- Never arrange a face-to-face meeting with someone they met online.
- Never upload or post pictures of themselves onto the Internet for people they do not personally know.
- Never give out identifying information, such as name, home address, school name, or telephone number.
- Never download pictures from an unknown source, as there is a good chance they could be sexually explicit images.
- Never respond to messages or bulletin board postings that are suggestive, obscene, belligerent, or harassing.
- Whatever they are told online may or may not be true.[9]

All Internet users can take steps to help protect themselves, such as keeping personal information as private as possible, using the privacy settings provided by social media sites, changing passwords frequently, not sharing passwords, and not sharing information online about a current location. Taking proactive steps can help reduce the chances of becoming a target.

More than One Side

Those who support censorship tend to be concerned citizens who fear that some materials may harm children or teach them things that could be harmful. Censored material often involves sexually related content, offensive language, or potentially dangerous information, such as how to make bombs. Following the shootings at Columbine High School in Littleton, Colorado, in 1998, many people became more concerned about the information available to minors on the Internet. Columbine killers Eric Harris and Dylan Klebold found information on the Internet that they used to make pipe bombs.[10]

Do you believe in free speech or censorship on the Internet? Once you begin debating the issue using real examples, you might see how the issue is more complex than it seems.

Supporters of censorship argue that tragedies such as this could be lessened if kids do not have access to this type of dangerous material.

Those who argue against censorship believe that people have the right to make their own choices about what they read and see. They also argue that it is not up to the authority of certain people, groups, or the government to determine what should be taught in schools. Sex and drug education, for example, often fall into censorship issues. Those who oppose such education believe that it will only teach children how to use drugs or encourage them to have sex. These groups recommend "just say no" drug campaigns and abstinence-only sex education programs. Those who oppose such censorship argue that some minors will experiment—or at least seek information—no matter what. Having accurate information gives them the tools they need to make wise decisions rather than relying on friends or assumptions. They argue, for example, that abstinence programs provide inaccurate or limited information on pregnancy and sexually transmitted diseases and therefore leave teens at a disadvantage.

Defending One's Rights

In the article "What You Can Do to Oppose Censorship," the ALA lists a number of things people can do to fight censorship.[11] Another organization, kidSPEAK!, lists ways in which minors can get involved to fight for intellectual freedom on their website page "What Can I Do?"[12] The following information is based on these lists.

For those who wish to oppose censorship—and not everyone does—a good place to start is the local library. Many libraries, including some school libraries, oppose censorship. Is it possible to fight censorship without breaking the law? Yes. Libraries do not support illegal activities. This includes exposing minors to inappropriate sexually explicit material. Nor do many libraries enforce the idea of censorship. Some help deal with the Internet issue by placing computers in the children's and young adult areas close to the librarians' desk. This discourages patrons from viewing inappropriate material in the children's section of the library. Knowing the importance of intellectual freedom and passing that knowledge on to others is one way to support intellectual freedom at the library.

Even though minors may not vote, they do have the right and ability to contact people in decision-making jobs and government officials about issues that are important to young people. Contacting library and school boards, local media, and elected officials is a way to get an opinion out there and be heard. If a school is considering censoring certain information, students can ask to speak at one of the school board meetings to express opinions—either opposing or supporting the idea. Writing letters to the school and local papers may also be an option. A letter to the editor is an easy, brief way to get an opinion heard.

Keeping informed about issues related to intellectual freedom is also important. Following the news is a way to get information about what is going on at the local, state, and national levels.

Many people, including many minors, support censorship of some material. The First Amendment grants the right to personal opinions for all people. Teens can apply all the tools listed here to any issue regarding freedom of expression. Regardless of opinions, maintaining current information on the issues is important. It is difficult to take a stand without knowing all sides of an issue. Contacting government officials, writing letters, and developing campaigns to support a goal are all methods used to make a public statement.

Many groups are dedicated to preserving intellectual freedom rights, regardless of the positions. These groups feel that all opinions and voices can and should be heard. Joining such a group is a good way to get involved. Starting a group is another option. If a school is debating censorship issues, forming a student group to discuss issues and speak out is one way to take action.

Termination of Parental Rights and Emancipation

Ideally, every child would grow up in a healthy, safe home. All children would have enough to eat, clean clothes, people who love and care for them, and opportunities to learn, read, and expand their interests at home. Unfortunately, this is far from reality for many children. All children do have the right to live free from abusive situations and to seek help when needed.

Too many children grow up in unsafe homes. They suffer abuse, neglect, poverty, and a lot of other problems. Some of the larger issues related to parental rights have to do with abuse and neglect. These are serious issues, and a teen who finds him- or herself in a troublesome situation has the right to seek help. Finding that help may seem difficult or scary, but it is available. One way these problems are sometimes handled is through termination of parental rights (TPR), in which a court takes away the parents' rights to make decisions about a child. Some forms of abuse that may lead to termination of parental rights are outlined below.[1]

Physical abuse of children can range from spanking to beatings and more. Parents do this sometimes out of anger, sometimes to punish a child, and sometimes for no obvious reason. The law allows some forms of corporal, or physical, punishment. Parents can take this too far and engage in abuse. Some cases of corporal punishment have gone to court. The rulings vary depending on each case. Some types of spanking, for example, are legal, and some are not.

According to one child advocacy organization, emotional abuse in the parent/child relationship occurs "when an adult continually hurts a child's feelings by calling names, using put downs, insults or humiliation."[2] Emotional abuse may not seem as serious as physical abuse. In reality, its effects can last a long time and be damaging.

Sexual abuse in the parent/child relationship or an adult/child relationship occurs when the adult engages in sexual activity with the child. In these situations, the older person pushes inappropriate, unwanted, nonconsensual sexual behavior on the child. This unwanted behavior can include touching, kissing, fondling, nudity, and intercourse. There is a difference in the amount of power held by the people in the relationship, with the adult holding power over the child.

Statutory rape occurs when one person over a given age has sex with a person under the age of consent. This is the age at which a person can legally consent to have sex, and it varies from state to state with sixteen being the most common. Even if the younger person agrees to have sex, it is still a form of rape under the law, and the older person may face charges.

Neglect occurs when a caretaker deprives a child of basic needs. This can include physical, emotional, or educational needs. Physical needs include such things as food, water, clothing, and shelter. Emotional needs are love, attention, and protection. According to US law, children also have a right to an education, which parents must meet.[3]

Children and teens have the right to live in a home in which their basic needs are met. Those who live with abuse should seek assistance from a school counselor or trusted adult.

An abused person needs to find help immediately. Help may be in the form of assistance from a friend or a person in authority. Report any abuse to someone who can help. A school counselor can help direct a teen to the proper resources, as can a clergy member or teacher. The state's Department of Health and Human Services can provide help. An Internet search will direct you to abuse hotlines that will help you.

Parental Rights and Responsibilities

Parents who abuse or neglect their children can face criminal charges and be forced to give up their parental rights. Sometimes parents will give up the rights to their children voluntarily. If the charges are serious enough, the parent or parents may go to jail for their actions. When a parent loses parental rights, the children need a new home.

Termination of parental rights is a legal procedure that makes adoption possible for the child or children without the consent of the birth parents. Before this occurs, children are sometimes put in foster care. This is when a family volunteers to care for a child until a permanent adoption can take place. Foster parents must go through a training program and be approved by the state. When children are in foster care, they remain in the foster care system until the state determines it is safe for them to return home. If it is not, the children will then be eligible for adoption. Sometimes foster parents adopt the children they have been caring for. Other relatives, such as grandparents or aunts and uncles, may take in the children, depending on the situation.

The laws on TPR vary greatly from state to state and the social welfare systems that each state has in place.

Care Options

If a teen is in trouble and needs to leave home for a night or for an extended period of time, there may be options depending on the community. Youth shelters, if available, may allow a teen to stay overnight but may require a parent's permission to do so. Children in serious trouble may be placed in temporary foster care until a long-term plan can be arranged if needed.

Speaking with a school counselor, trusted adult, or member of the clergy may help a teen determine possible solutions for seeking help. An Internet search or even the yellow pages in your local phone book may list local community groups that work with minors. See adolescents and related terms, or look under counseling.

Leaving Home Early

Most teens have probably thought about divorcing their parents at one time or another. While the idea may sound like a perfect solution, the reality is quite different. The term emancipation is often confused with the true meaning. It is not exactly like getting a divorce.

Under normal circumstances, parents are responsible for their child until he or she reaches the legal age. When a minor is emancipated, it means that his or her parents are no longer legally responsible for the minor. In other words, the parent is no longer responsible for providing food, shelter, health care, education, or any other basic needs. The parent has no legal or financial obligations to an emancipated child. An emancipated teen is legally responsible for him- or herself. The law views the minor as an adult.

A judge will not grant emancipation just because a teen does not like the rules at home. The courts grant parents a lot of freedom when it comes to raising children. Unless a child is in danger, he or she is subject to the parents' rules until reaching legal age. Emancipation can occur a few different ways before a person reaches eighteen. A minor can marry (laws vary state by state in regards to age), join the military, or obtain a court order by proving that he or she is living on his or her own and is financially independent. The court will review all the information and make a decision.

Some states, such as California, offer simplified procedures for emancipation. These allow for parental consent and speed up the process. The minor must show that he or she is at least fourteen years of age, is financially independent, and is living apart from his or her parents. While this process is easier, an emancipated teen may be more likely to end up homeless or drop out of school. Emancipation is a decision that requires serious thought. It may be the right choice for some but not all.

An emancipated teen faces schoolwork, employment, rent, medical expenses—which are particularly high, especially if no insurance is available—utilities . . . the list goes on. Even some people over the age of eighteen do not face all of these issues immediately after reaching the legal age. Many parents support their children into their twenties and sometimes afterward.

Minors who wish to be legally emancipated from their parents must be able to provide for themselves and prove that they are better off on their own than in the care of their parents.

Becoming an Adult

What exactly does emancipation mean? It means that a minor is an adult according to the law. Does the minor have all the same rights as an adult? Not quite. Minors must still follow the law. A teen may not purchase tobacco products or drink until reaching the legal age. An emancipated minor cannot vote. Emancipated teens must also follow child labor laws.

How does one start the emancipation process? The child files an emancipation petition or has a lawyer file the petition. A judge reviews the case and makes a final decision. Emancipation usually cannot be undone, so careful consideration is required. Talking with a counselor or lawyer may help a teen make a sound decision.

When Teens Break the Law

Minors are still citizens, and as such, they are subject to the laws of their state and the federal government. The consequences of breaking some laws may be more severe for a person who is eighteen or older, but minors can still face serious consequences if they break the law. Those laws vary from state to state, and charges for breaking those laws range from infractions, or petty offenses that may come with fines but not jail time; to misdemeanors, up to a year in jail; and felonies, the most serious offenses.[1] Minors can be charged with any of these types of offenses, and in some situations, they may be charged as adults. The following information is an overview of some general legal information that affects teens.

The US Constitution allows each state to determine its own laws. The only rule is that the laws must be in compliance with the Constitution. As a result, punishment for the same crime can differ from state to state. The age at which a minor may be tried as an adult for a crime may also vary. One state may charge the offender as a juvenile while another state may charge the offender as an adult for the same crime.

Minors have rights under the US Constitution. However, their rights are more restricted than those of adults. For example, minors cannot vote or sign contracts. While the Bill of Rights guarantees the freedom of speech, minors do not always have this right—for instance, when they are in school.

Until recently, minors who were charged with breaking the law had few of the due process protections given to adults. For instance, they did not have the right to have an attorney, to confront their accusers in court, to have a jury trial, to refuse to testify in their trial, or to appeal a verdict. This was because the purpose of the youth court system was to rehabilitate and teach young people rather than punish them. Experts believed that this would be more likely in an informal system in which judges had a great deal of discretion to decide cases and sentences.

In 1964, a fifteen-year-old boy in Arizona named Gerald Gault was arrested for making a prank phone call including indecent remarks to a neighbor. Gault was never read his rights, was never formally charged, did not have an attorney at his hearing, and was not allowed to confront his accuser in court. Despite all this, Gault was tried and sentenced to six years in a state juvenile detention facility. The case was eventually appealed to the Supreme Court, which ruled for Gault in 1967. The Court said that because children who are charged with crimes faced many of the same consequences as adults, they should have the same right to due process.

The Juvenile Court System

Currently, a teen has the same legal rights as an adult during the arrest process. The Miranda warning is read by the police to suspects during an arrest. This is the list of rights heard in television shows

A police offer must read you your Miranda rights during an arrest. Otherwise, the case may be dismissed. Knowing your legal rights can make all the difference if you are arrested.

and movies that begins, "You have the right to remain silent." If police do not read a suspect these rights, a judge may dismiss a case.

Juvenile court is a separate legal system that deals with legal issues affecting minors. In most states, the juvenile court system deals with those up to the age of eighteen. The juvenile court handles many issues. These include adoption, abuse and neglect, mental and physical health issues such as abortion, and delinquency or misbehavior. When the juvenile court hears delinquency cases where a minor is charged with breaking the law, in most cases the court will attempt to address the problem. Rehabilitation in the court system refers to processes that help people charged with a crime change their ways and become productive members of society.

Even in the most serious cases, such as a murder trial, a juvenile court will likely determine if rehabilitation is a possibility. This takes place before trying the juvenile or determining if the minor will be tried in juvenile or adult court. Some states, however, have a system in place that automatically places a case in the adult court. This means that some states will try a juvenile in an adult court for murder or other serious crimes without considering other factors. In Wisconsin, for example, a law requires that children aged ten to sixteen who are charged with certain types of homicide are automatically sent to adult court.[2]

The preferred course of action for juveniles convicted of crimes is rehabilitation. This can mean time in a detention center, but it can also mean required counseling or community service.

Being tried in juvenile court, however, does not mean a minor will automatically get off easy for committing a crime. Sentences in a juvenile court range from jail time to probation. Probation is a system that allows a guilty person to stay out of jail and report to a probation officer instead. Breaking the rules of probation can lead to imprisonment.[3]

Locked Up

When teens are required to serve jail time, they usually go to a juvenile ward. Time in a juvenile ward differs from time in a regular jail. Time is devoted to the rehabilitative process.[4] Serving time in one of these places is not easy. It just means that the focus is different. It also keeps minors away from adult offenders who are serving time.

Juveniles can serve time in adult prisons if found guilty of serious crimes. A 2000 report published by the US Department of Justice states:

> Concerned that the juvenile justice system may be ill equipped to handle youth charged with serious crimes and that the juvenile court may be too lenient in its punishment and control of such youth, many states have begun amending their criminal codes so that youth charged with certain crimes can be tried in adult courts and sentenced as adults.[5]

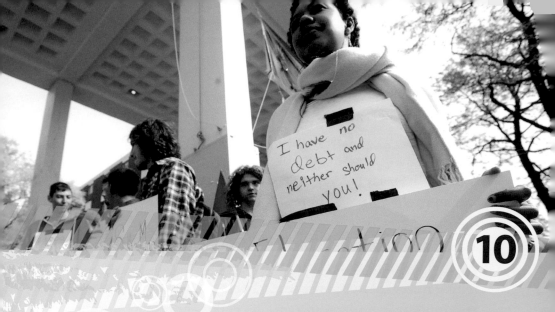

Where Does This Leave Teens?

M any issues affect teens, and this resource covers only a few. More information is available to teens now than ever before, and many teens are taking actions on issues that are important to them. With social media, websites geared toward younger people, and other means of communication, teens are able to speak out, share their views on important issues, and make themselves heard. Teens' voices can affect policies, politics, and social change. These can include topics such as gun violence, LGBT rights, freedom of religion, human rights, and many more.

It is a citizen's responsibility to know what his or her rights are. Without this knowledge, a person will not know if they are being violated. He or she may also violate the rights of another. Having rights includes respecting the rights of others.

No one can know all of the laws inside and out—even attorneys have to do legal research—but having a basic understanding of the Constitution and the Bill of Rights helps ensure respect for all citizens' rights. The right to speak out is most effective when it is used intelligently. Having knowledge of basic human rights can help a person spot a violation of another's rights. It could even save someone else's life. Children's rights supporters feel strongly about their role in helping to speak for those who cannot. The same idea applies to everyday citizens. Knowledge is power. Being aware of various methods that some people use to exploit others can go a long way toward stopping abuses. For instance, knowing the signs of child abuse can lead toward getting a child proper help. Not allowing another person or company to take advantage of minors can lead to better human rights practices all around.

As with anything, keeping informed and taking action are ways to help ensure that rights remain constitutionally protected and enforced. For those who seek change, taking action is the best way to deal with issues. Even for those who do not wish to take up a cause, knowing one's rights and keeping informed is necessary to fully function in school and in society.

Children in the United States have many rights that children around the world do not. Around the globe, many crimes are committed against children. Even so, children's rights are still sometimes abused in the United States. Knowing about rights abuse is one thing. Doing something about it is another.

Young people do have options when it comes to taking action. Starting a rights group at school is one possibility. Getting involved in a local or national human rights group is another. Many organizations have information on the Internet about joining their organization, as well as tips on starting a local group.

Writing articles and opinion pieces for both school and local papers is one way to discuss issues and draw attention to a problem. Writing local, state, and national decision makers is another way people get their voices heard. Even though minors cannot vote, they still have voices and can use them. Politicians are supposed to represent the people at large, not one particular group over another. Minors are important members of society.

Volunteering is another way to help support human rights activities. Check into local nonprofit groups for those who work for similar beliefs. Help others or work for a cause by volunteering.

While many people are working to speak for those who cannot speak for themselves, oftentimes youth rights begin with youths. If a young person had not bothered to challenge the law, many youth rights would not be in place today. At times it may seem that minors do not have many rights. Some areas of the law will not change. But there is always room for some change, and there is only one way to go make change happen—by doing something about it.

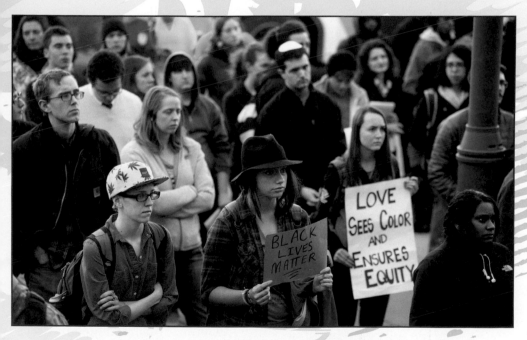

In the United States, having a basic grasp of your constitutional rights can give you the confidence to speak up for yourself and others. You might even enact change for the better.

Chapter Notes

Chapter 1: What Are Your Rights?

1. "Fourth Amendment—U.S. Constitution—FindLaw." *Findlaw*, Findlaw, n.d., Web, 28 June 2015.
2. "United States Court of Appeals." *International Legal Materials* 20.3 (1981): 637-38, Web, <http://www.ca6.uscourts.gov/opinions.pdf/13a0078p-06.pdf>.
3. John Shattuck, "Civil and Political Rights in the United States," US Department of State Dispatch, September 19, 1994, <http://www.findarticles.com/p/articles/mi_m1584/is_n38_v5/ai_15930215> (February 20, 2005).
4. Free The Children, "Children's Rights, Who Has Ratified?" 2003, <http://www.freethechildren.org/youthinaction/children's_rights_who_has_ratified.htm> (February 28, 2004).

Chapter 2: The Right to Free Speech

1. Tinker v. Des Moines School Dist., 393 U.S. 503 (1969) 393 U.S. 503 Tinker et al. v. Des Moines Independent Community School District et al., Certiorari to the United States Court of Appeals for the Eighth Circuit, No. 21. Argued November 12, 1968, <http://caselaw.lp.findlaw.com/scripts/getcase.pl?navby=case&court=US&vol=393&page=503> (February 29, 2004).
2. Torres, Alec, "High School Student Suspended for Wearing NRA Shirt." *National Review Online.* The Corner, 12 Mar. 2014, Web, 28 June 2015, <http://www.nationalreview.com/corner/373216/high-school-student-suspended-wearing-nra-shirt-alec-torres>.
3. Hazelwood School District v. Kuhlmeier, 484 US 260 (1988),

<http://www.wku.edu/Government/vhazel.htm> (February 23, 2004).

4. Oyez, U. S. Supreme Court Multimedia, "Engel v. Vitale," n.d., <www.oyez.org/oyez/resource/case/111/abstract> (February 19, 2005).

5. FindLaw, "Engel v. Vitale," n.d., <http://caselaw.lp.findlaw.com/ scripts/getcase.pl?court=US&vol=370&invol=421> (February 20, 2005).

6. Engel v. Vitale, 370 U.S. 421 (1962), <http://www.civnet.org/ resources/teach/basic/part7/47.htm> (February 23, 2004).

7. Lee v. Weisman, 505 U.S. 577 (1992), Section (a), <http:// tourolaw.edu/patch/Lee>.

8. Ibid., Section (b).

9. "Chisholm Student Expelled over Facebook 'hit List'" *Duluth News Tribune*. Duluth News Tribune, 24 Mar. 2011, Web, 28 June 2015, <http://www.duluthnewstribune.com/content/ chisholm-student-expelled-over-facebook-hit-list>.

10. Holloway, Hailey, "Blount County Teen Suspended More than a Year over Twitter Conversation." *WATE 6 On Your Side*, Wate.com, 03 Feb. 2015, Web, 28 June 2015, <http://wate. com/2015/02/03/blount-county-teen-suspended-more-than-a-year-over-twitter-conversation/>.

11. Levy, Paul, "Rogers High Student Sues District over Fallout from Online Post." *Star Tribune*. Star Tribune, 20 June 2014, Web, 28 June 2015, <http://www.startribune.com/ rogers-high-student-sues-district-over-fallout-from-online-post/263479661/>.

12. "What Is Cyberbullying." *What Is Cyberbullying*, Stopbullying. gov, n.d., Web, 28 June 2015, <http://www.stopbullying.gov/ cyberbullying/what-is-it/index.html>.

13. "What Is Cyberbullying." *What Is Cyberbullying*, Stopbullying.

gov, n.d., Web, 28 June 2015, <http://www.stopbullying.gov/cyberbullying/what-is-it/index.html>.

14. "Warning Signs." *Warning Signs*, Stopbullying.gov, n.d., Web, 28 June 2015, <http://www.stopbullying.gov/at-risk/warning-signs/index.html>.

Chapter 3: Rights at Work

1. Steven Mitchell Sack, *The Employee Rights Handbook* (Warner Books: New York, 2000), pp. 9–14.

2. "Table 1. Labor Force Status of 2014 High School Graduates and 2013-14 High School Dropouts 16 to 24 Years Old by School Enrollment, Educational Attainment, Sex, Race, and Hispanic or Latino Ethnicity, October 2014." *US Bureau of Labor Statistics*, US Bureau of Labor Statistics, 19 May 2015, Web, 30 June 2015, <http://www.bls.gov/news.release/hsgec.t01.htm>.

3. "BLS 2013 Workplace Fatality Data." *Commonly Used Statistics*. US Department of Labor, n.d., Web, 30 June 2015, <https://www.osha.gov/oshstats/commonstats.html>.

4. National Consumers League, "Clocking in for Trouble: Teens and Unsafe Work," n.d., <http://www.natlconsumersleague.org/childlabor/jobreport.htm> (December 8, 2004).

5. DHHS (NIOSH) Publication No. 97-132.

Chapter 4: Purchasing Power

1. Alissa Quart, *Branded: The Buying and Selling of Teenagers* (Cambridge, Mass.: Perseus Publishing, 2003), p. 98.

2. "Parental Escort Policy - Mall of America." Parental Escort Policy - Mall of America, Mall of America, n.d., Web, 30 June 2015, <http://www.mallofamerica.com/guests/escorts>.

3. Rosalind Bentley and Terry Collins, "Teens: the lifeblood and headache of the mall," Startribune.com, n.d., <http://www.

startribune.com/stories/1731/3137749-2.html> (December 8, 2004).

4. David A. Walsh and Douglas A. Gentile, "A Validity Test of Movie, Television, and Video-Game Ratings," Pediatrics, vol. 107, no. 6, June 2001, p. 1302.

5. Ibid.

6. Teen Consumer Scrapbook, "CD Parent Advisory Labels," n.d., <http://www.atg.wa.gov/teenconsumer/buyingG&S/cdlabels.htm> (February 23, 2004).

7. Federal Trade Commission, "Marketing Violent Entertainment to Children," July 12, 2004, <http://www.ftc.gov/os/2004/07/040708kidsviolencerpt.pdf> (December 10, 2004).

8. Ibid., p. 28.

9. Teen Consumer Scrapbook, "Consumer Complaints," n.d., <www.atg.wa.gov/teenconsumer/pages/buyingG&S/consumercomp.htm> (February 20, 2005).

Chapter 5: Health and Well-Being

1. Jefferson County Department of Health, Birmingham, Alabama, "Teens' Consumer Health Rights," n.d., <http://www.jcdh.org/default.asp?ID=128> (February 28, 2004).

2. The Alan Guttmacher Institute, "Parental Involvement in Minors' Abortion," State Policies in Brief, as of December 1, 2004, <http://www.guttmacher.org/statecenter/spibs/spib_PIMA.pdf> (December 11, 2004).

3. Rebecca Gudeman, "Federal Privacy Protection for Substance Abuse Treatment Records: Protecting Adolescents," July–September 2003, <http://www.youthlaw.org/downloads/substance_abuse_records.pdf> (December 11, 2004).

Chapter 6: Drug Testing and Searches

1. Vernonia School District v. Acton, 515 U.S. 646 (1995),

<http://www.oyez.org/oyez/resource/case/626/> (January 11, 2005).

2. Office of National Drug Control Policy, "What You Need to Know About Drug Testing in Schools," n.d., <http://www. whitehousedrugpolicy.gov/pdf/drug_testing.pdf> (February 23, 2004).

3. "Schools' Authority on Dispensing Medication - FindLaw." *Findlaw*, Findlaw, 2014, Web, 30 June 2015, <http:// education.findlaw.com/school-safety/schools-authority-on-dispensing-medication.html>.

Chapter 7: Unlimited Data

1. American Library Association, "Intellectual Freedom and Censorship Q&A," n.d., <http://www.ala.org/ala/oif/basics/ intellectual.htm#ifpoint1> (January 11, 2005).

2. American Library Association, "CPPA, COPA, CIPA: Which Is Which?" 2004, <http://www.ala.org/ala/oif/ifissues/ issuesrelatedlinks/cppacopacipa.htm> (December 13, 2004).

3. "Children's Internet Protection Act." Children's Internet Protection Act, Federal Communications Commission, 31 Dec. 2014, Web, 27 June 2015, <https://www.fcc.gov/guides/ childrens-internet-protection-act>.

4. "Intellectual Freedom and Censorship Q & A." *Intellectual Freedom and Censorship Q & A*. American Library Association, n.d., Web, 27 June 2015, <http://www.ala.org/ advocacy/intfreedom/censorshipfirstamendmentissues/ ifcensorshipqanda>.

5. FindLaw, "U.S. Constitution: Ninth Amendment," n.d., <http://caselaw.lp.findlaw.com/data/constitution/ amendment09/#f5> (February 20, 2005).

6. Board Of Education v. Pico, 457 U.S. 853 (1982), abstract, n.d., <http://www.oyez.org/oyez/resource/case/1060/>

(December 13, 2004).

7. Ibid.
8. "Children's Online Privacy Protection Rule ("COPPA")." Children's Online Privacy Protection Rule ("COPPA"). Federal Trade Commission, n.d., Web, 28 June 2015, <https://www.ftc.gov/enforcement/rules/rulemaking-regulatory-reform-proceedings/childrens-online-privacy-protection-rule>.
9. "A Parent's Guide to Internet Safety." FBI, FBI, 03 June 2005, Web, 28 June 2015, <https://www.fbi.gov/stats-services/publications/parent-guide>.
10. "Did Cops Miss Columbine Tip?" CBSNews.com, October 30, 2003, <http://www.cbsnews.com/stories/2004/02/26/national/main602339.shtml> (December 13, 2004).
11. American Library Association, "What You Can Do to Oppose Censorship," n.d., <http://www.ala.org/Template.cfm?Section=basics&Template=/ContentManagement/ContentDisplay.cfm&ContentID=24792> (February 28, 2004).
12. kidSPEAK!, "What Can I Do?" <http://www.kidspeakonline.org/whatcanido.html> (February 29, 2004).

Chapter 8: Termination of Parental Rights and Emancipation

1. Laurie A. Couture, "General Information on Child Abuse and Neglect: Types of Abuse and Neglect," ChildAdvocate.org, 2003, <http://www.childadvocate.org/1d_types.htm> (February 29, 2004).
2. Ibid., <http://www.childadvocate.org/4c.htm> (February 29, 2004).
3. Ibid.

Chapter 9: When Teens Break the Law

1. "Felonies, Misdemeanors, and Infractions: Classifying Crimes Nolo.com."*Nolo.com.* Nolo Law for All, n.d., Web, 30 June 2015, <http://www.nolo.com/legal-encyclopedia/crimes-felonies-misdemeanors-infractions-classification-33814.html>.

2. Milwaukee Journal Sentinel, "Suspect, 10, May Become the Youngest Ever Charged," October 3, 2002, <http://www.cjcj.org/press/suspect.html> (December 13, 2004).

3. Legal Dictionary online, "probation," 2003–2004, <http://www.thelegaldictionary.com/legal-term-details/Probation> (December 13, 2004).

4. Center on Juvenile and Criminal Justice, "Intro to California's Juvenile Justice System; Life as a Juvenile Ward," n.d., <http://www.cjcj.org/jjic/intro.php#ljw> (December 13, 2004).

5. US Department of Justice, Office of Justice Programs, Bureau of Justice Assistance, James Austin, Kelly Dedel Johnson, Maria Gregoriou, Institute on Crime, Justice and Corrections at The George Washington University and National Council on Crime and Delinquency, "Juveniles in Adult Prisons and Jails, A National Assessment," October 2000, <http://www.ncjrs.org/pdffiles1/bja/182503.pdf> (December 13, 2004).

Glossary

amendment—An article added to the US Constitution.

article—A separate clause or portion of a document.

Better Business Bureau—Agency that reports wrongful business practices.

Bill of Rights—The first ten amendments to the Constitution.

censor—A person who examines printed matter, movies, news, etc. to suppress parts on the grounds of obscenity, security, etc.

contraceptives—Means and methods to prevent pregnancy.

Convention on the Rights of the Child (CRC)—A list of articles developed by the United Nations in 1989 outlining rights specific to children.

Children's Online Privacy Protection Act (COPPA)—A law created to help protect the privacy of children under the age of thirteen.

defamation of character—A false statement that is intended to damage another person's character or otherwise cause harm.

due process—The principle that the state must use fair procedures when it acts to limit a person's life, liberty, or property.

emancipation—Becoming legal in the eyes of the law before reaching the legal age of eighteen.

ERSB—Rating standard-setting body for video games.

Fair Labor Standards Act—The 1938 legislation that dictated areas of labor law, including child labor.

Federal Trade Commission (FTC)—The US government agency that deals with consumer issues.

harass—To trouble and annoy continually.

hate speech—Hateful or derogatory speech aimed at another person or group of people; it is directed at people because of membership in a minority group, sexual orientation, etc.

Internet filters—Programs designed to block users from viewing websites containing certain words.

minor—Anyone under the state-defined legal age.

Occupational Safety and Health Administration (OSHA)—A US government agency that regulates workplace safety.

ratify—To confirm or accept by formal consent, signature, etc.

Recording Industry Association of America (RIAA)—The organization that developed the Parental Advisory Label for explicit lyrics in music.

sexual harassment—Harassment involving sexual language, touching, or other inappropriate sexually related behavior.

slander—A false and hurtful statement about another.

Supreme Court—Highest court in the United States, which deals with constitutional issues.

Universal Declaration of Human Rights (UDHR)—Declaration of the United Nations put into effect in 1948 that lists basic human rights.

For More Information

American Civil Liberties Union
25 Broad Street, 18th Floor
New York, NY 10004
(212) 549-2500
aclu.org

The American Library Association
50 E. Huron
Chicago IL 60611
(800) 545-2433
www.ala.org

Center on Juvenile and Criminal Justice
1234 Massachusetts Avenue NW
Suite C1009
Washington, DC 20005
(202) 737-7270
cjcj.org/index.html

Centers for Disease Control and Prevention
1600 Clifton Road
Atlanta, GA 30333
(800) 311-3435
cdc.gov

National Coalition Against Censorship
275 Seventh Avenue
New York, NY 10001
(212) 807-6222
ncac.org

National Youth Rights Association

PO Box 5882 NW
Washington, DC 20016
(301) 738-6769
youthrights.org

Occupational Safety & Health Administration

200 Constitution Avenue NW
Washington, DC 20210
(800) 321-OSHA
osha.gov

Youth Rights

Amnesty International USA
5 Penn Plaza, 14th Floor
New York, NY 10001
(212) 807-8400
amnestyusa.org/resources/students-and-youth

Websites

Children's Rights

childrensrights.org

An organization whose mission is "Defending America's Abused and Neglected Kids."

StopBullying.gov

stopbullying.gov/index.html

A US government website dedicated to ending bullying.

Stomp Out Bullying

stompoutbullying.org

"The leading national anti-bullying and cyberbullying organization for kids and teens in the U.S."

Further Reading

Bazelon, Emily. *Sticks and Stones: Defeating the Culture of Bullying and Rediscovering the Power of Character and Empathy*. New York: Random House, 2014.

Covey, Sean. *The 7 Habits of Highly Effective Teens*. New York: Touchstone, 2014.

Hudson Jr., David L. *Teen Legal Rights*, 3rd Edition. Santa Barbrara, Calif.: Greenwood, 2015.

Jacobs, Thomas A. *What are My Rights? Q&A About Teens and the Law*. Minneapolis, Minn.: Free Spirit Publishing, 2011.

Kootz, Russel, and David Seidman. *Understanding Your Civil Rights*. New York: Rosen Publishing, 2012.

Merino, Noël. *Privacy*. Farmington Hills, Mich.: Greenhaven Press, 2015.

Index

A

abortion, 49, 52–55, 90

abuse, 49, 50, 53, 69, 81–83, 90, 94

Acton, Jimmy, 58

adoption, 84, 90

adult court, 91–92

adult offenders, 89, 92

advertising, 37–38, 41, 45

African Americans, 6

age and work, 30, 32–33

alcohol use, 50, 53

American Civil Liberties Union (ACLU), 45, 62, 70

American Library Association (ALA), 69, 71, 79

athletics and drug testing, 58, 60

B

banned books, 74

Better Business Bureau, 36, 47

Bill of Rights, 12, 89, 94

birth control, 52, 72, 74

C

censorship, 45, 72, 74, 75–76, 78–80

child labor, 30, 32, 34–35, 87

Child Online Protection Act (COPA), 70

Children's Internet Protection Act (CIPA), 70,

Children's Online Privacy Protection Act (COPPA), 70, 76

Columbine High School, 45, 78

Communications Decency Act (CDA), 70

confidentiality and medical records, 53, 54

Constitution, 10, 12–13, 72, 88–89, 94

consumer laws, 39, 41, 43 45–46

contraceptives, 50

Convention on the Rights of the Child (CRC), 9–10

corporal punishment, 82

D

death penalty, 10

defamation of character, 15

detention, 89

drug education, 57, 66–67, 79

drug searches, 57, 59, 62

drug testing, 57–60, 62–63, 64, 66–67

drug use, 53, 57, 58–59

due process, 62, 64, 89